HOW TO WIN AN ARGUMENT

HOW TO WIN
AN ARGUMENT

■ ■ ■ ■ ■ ■

An Ancient Guide to the Art of Persuasion

Marcus Tullius Cicero

*Selected, Edited, and Translated
by James M. May*

PRINCETON UNIVERSITY PRESS

PRINCETON AND OXFORD

Published by Princeton University Press, 41 William Street,
Princeton, New Jersey 08540
In the United Kingdom: Princeton University Press, 6 Oxford
Street, Woodstock, Oxfordshire OX20 1TR

press.princeton.edu

Jacket art: Ancient marble portrait bust.
Courtesy of Shutterstock © Gilmanshin.

Library of Congress Cataloging-in-Publication Data

Names: Cicero, Marcus Tullius, author. | May, James M.,
editor, translator.
Title: How to win an argument : an ancient guide to the art
of persuasion / Marcus Tullius Cicero ; selected, edited, and
translated by James M. May.
Description: Princeton ; Oxford : Princeton University Press,
2016. | Includes bibliographical references.
Identifiers: LCCN 2016012361 | ISBN 9780691164335 (hardcover
: alk. paper)
Subjects: LCSH: Rhetoric, Ancient. | Persuasion (Rhetoric) |
Cicero, Marcus Tullius.
Classification: LCC PA6307.A2 M39 2016 | DDC 808—dc23
LC record available at http://lccn.loc.gov/2016012361

British Library Cataloging-in-Publication Data is available

This book has been composed in Stemple Garamond and Futura

Printed on acid-free paper. ∞

Printed in the United States of America

5 7 9 10 8 6

CONTENTS

CONTENTS

PREFACE

For as long as human beings have had the ability to communicate, we have endeavored to persuade one another. Whether it be for the purposes of mere survival, or to control the circumstances of our lives, or to bring someone around to our way of thinking, or merely to win an argument, we have relied on some form of persuasion—either physical force or, what we would consider more "civilized" means, speaking and writing —to accomplish our goals and purposes. The art of verbal persuasion, in a word "rhetoric," was discovered in the West in the democracies of Syracuse and Athens during the fifth century BC. Citizens in democratic societies were expected to express themselves in assembly, represent themselves in courts of law, and participate in other civic functions. As a result, in order to enable people to operate successfully in society, attempts were made to describe effective means of verbal persuasion, and a theoretical system evolved that enabled citizens to plan and execute a successful speech in public—in other words, to win an argument.

Several centuries later, Rome's greatest orator and one of the greatest speakers of all time, Marcus Tullius Cicero, secured Rome's highest political office, the consulship, having relied heavily on this art of verbal persuasion to make a name for himself in Roman society. Trained from boyhood in the technicalities of rhetoric, Cicero excelled not only as an effective public speaker, who won the vast majority of arguments in which he was involved, but also as a theorist in the art of verbal persuasion, having written during his lifetime several treatises that have rhetoric as their subject. And although he is highly critical of the typical rhetorical handbooks of the day, he was, nonetheless, steeped in their doctrine and reliant upon their methods. In fact, this rhetorical education for civic duty, handed down by the Greeks and adopted by the Romans, remained a primary element in the training of all educated people throughout the Middle Ages, into the Renaissance, and even down into modern times.

Given the centrality of rhetoric, that is, the art of verbal persuasion, in our Western tradition, I present here a short anthology of passages from Cicero's writings, primarily his rhetorical treatises, that capture the essence of this ancient rhetorical system of persuasion, a system that helped to make Cicero and countless other orators effective speakers, able to convince people and win arguments. Readers will, I hope, find these selections interesting in their own right, as well as useful when thinking about their own efforts to persuade. Indeed, whether arguing with a friend over a trivial issue or presenting a brief before the Supreme Court, the goal of a speaker is still to persuade, and knowing the most effective means of persuasion in any given circumstance will lead to the successful realization of that goal. A peculiar paradox of contemporary American society is that, at a time when we find many schools, colleges, and universities talking seriously about fostering oral competency and good communication skills in their students, we actually see very few effective public speakers in action, in the courts, in our communities, or in the public arena of political life. While this book is certainly not intended to remedy that situation, my hope is that those who think about speaking in public and want to win arguments will find it appealing, and will delight in the realization that the techniques for effective oral persuasion discovered and enunciated millennia ago still make sense and have great relevance for those who would speak convincingly today.

In order to simplify matters and allow for smoother reading, I have avoided appending footnotes to names and terms that might present challenges to readers who are unfamiliar with the historical period or the technical subject matter. In lieu of such notes, a glossary of names and terms has been included near the end of the volume to which the reader can refer when seeking more detailed information or clarification. In addition, a list of suggestions for further reading on the subject has also been appended, consisting of both primary works by Cicero in English translation as well as secondary works that elucidate and comment upon ancient rhetoric and oratory, Cicero, and his works. All translations, except those from *De oratore*, are my own. *De oratore* passages were previously translated jointly by my colleague, Jakob Wisse, and me, and appeared originally in our complete translation of the treatise, published by Oxford University Press in 2001, *Cicero: On the Ideal Orator.* Occasionally, I have altered a word or two of that original translation in the passages that appear here.

I would like to thank Mr. Robert Tempio, executive editor and Humanities Group publisher for Princeton University Press, for suggesting this volume to me, and for his guidance and direction in seeing it through to publication; and Sara Lerner, senior production editor. I owe a debt of gratitude also to my copyeditor, Jennifer Harris, and to the anonymous referees of the Press, whose corrections, observations, and suggestions improved the manuscript greatly. I dedicate this little book to Augustus James May, in the hopes that, as he grows in age and wisdom, he will realize the ideal of the Elder Cato, becoming a *vir bonus dicendi peritus* ("a good man, skilled in speaking").

James M. May
St. Olaf College

CICERO'S LIFE: A BRIEF SKETCH

Marcus Tullius Cicero was born on 3 January, 106 BC, in Arpinum, a town approximately 70 miles southeast of Rome to a family that, though not members of the Roman nobility, was prominent in the local community and had important connections in the capital. While Marcus and his brother, Quintus, were still boys, the family moved to Rome, a move aimed at advancing the education and prospects of the brothers; there the boys were brought into contact with the two leading orators of the day, Lucius Licinius Crassus and Marcus Antonius, who were later to become the two chief speakers in Cicero's greatest rhetorical treatise, a dialogue on the ideal orator, *De oratore*. In such an environment, from boyhood on, Cicero was able to observe Rome's leading speakers and statesmen operating on a daily basis in the courts and in the forum. After Crassus's death in 91 BC, Cicero, at the age of

15 or 16, assumed the "toga of manhood" and was formally introduced to Quintus Mucius Scaevola, "the Augur," one of Rome's greatest legal experts (who is also given a place as one of the speakers in *De oratore*); under his tutelage, Cicero acquired his enormous respect and knowledge of the civil law.

The young Cicero was, no doubt, a precocious student; in addition to his oratorical and legal studies with Crassus, Antonius, and Scaevola, he developed an interest in and abiding love for philosophy. While still a teenager, he published his first rhetorical work, *De inventione*, or *On Invention*, which in later years he would describe as "the sketchy and unsophisticated work that found its way out of my notebooks when I was a boy, or rather a youth" (*De oratore* 1.5), though even that work continued to exert a tremendous influence on rhetorical and oratorical studies throughout the Middle Ages into the Renaissance.

After a brief tour of military service during the War with the Italian Allies, Cicero returned to a Rome that, during the decade of the 80s BC, was largely torn apart by civil strife, bloodshed, and proscription, brought on by the conflict between the strong-arms Marius, Cinna, and Sulla. When some sense of order had finally been restored and the courts began to function again regularly, Cicero took up his first civil cases, to be followed in 80 BC by his first criminal case, his defense of Roscius of Ameria on a charge of parricide. Shortly after this impressive victory, he decided to continue his education by spending about two years on what amounted to a "grand tour" of Greece, where he met, interacted, and studied with several prestigious rhetoricians, orators, and philosophers. He returned to Rome in 77 BC, a more vigorous and refined speaker.

Cicero was now nearly 30 years old, the minimum age requirement for standing for the office of quaestor, a sort of public treasurer or paymaster. As mentioned earlier, his family was not numbered among the Roman nobility—none of them before him had become a Roman senator by virtue of being elected to public office. Thus, as a so-called new man (*novus homo*), Cicero found himself in a notably disadvantaged political position, seeing that election to the higher magistracies at Rome was jealously guarded by, and generally restricted to, members of this nobility of rank. Nonetheless, he managed to win the election, finishing first on the ballot and in his first eligible year, and served as quaestor in Sicily. The connections he forged there accrued to his benefit five years later, when the Sicilians, recalling his good and upright service, enlisted him to prosecute Gaius Verres, the corrupt governor of the island from 73–70 BC, on a charge of extortion. His stunning success in the case, against the power of the senatorial order and Hortensius, the most famous advocate of the day who was defending Verres, catapulted Cicero into the limelight as Rome's leading orator and advocate. Other political offices followed for Cicero—aedile, praetor, and finally consul, the highest magistracy in republican Rome.

During the final months of Cicero's year as consul in 63 BC, he uncovered a plot to overthrow the government, led by a revolutionary, bankrupt senator of noble descent, Lucius Sergius Catiline. Through his diligence, the assistance of informants, and his inspiring oratory (students of Latin will be familiar with the justly famous *Catilinarian Orations*), Cicero managed to thwart the coup and, with the threat still imminent, to gain approval of the Senate, over the objections of some, for execution of the conspirators without a trial. In the aftermath, a public thanksgiving was decreed and Cicero was hailed as *Pater Patriae*, "Father of the Fatherland."

In this moment of triumph, when he had seemingly managed to unite the Roman people against the threat of the coup, Cicero envisioned a harmony among the various social classes of Rome (*concordia ordinum*). Only a few years later, however, forces would conspire to dash that dream and to transform the source of Cicero's crowning glory into one of debilitating disgrace. In 60 BC, various maneuverings and political machinations had fostered an alliance between three powerful men, Julius Caesar, the great general Pompey, and the wealthy Marcus Crassus, a distant relative of Cicero's boyhood mentor. Although initially invited to join the coalition, Cicero ultimately could not bring himself to support this so-called First Triumvirate, and they, in turn, were content to give free rein to his opponents, chief of whom was his arch-enemy, the tribune Publius Clodius, who managed to force him into exile in 58 BC, for executing Roman citizens without a trial. Taking refuge in Greece, Cicero endured the most miserable year and a half of his life, during which he suffered acute depression and even contemplated suicide. The Senate recalled him in triumph in 57 BC, but the triumvirs still held sway in Rome, and had warned Cicero (through the agency of his brother, Quintus) not to pursue any policy hostile to their interests; in fact, at the behest of the triumvirs he was even forced against his will to defend several of his former enemies. In this sort of repressive environment, Cicero turned to writing and spent the last several years of the decade composing some of his most important and significant literary treatises, including *De oratore (On the Ideal Orator)*, *De republica (On the Republic)*, and *De legibus (On the Laws)*.

In 51 BC, Cicero was assigned by the Senate to serve as proconsul of the province of Cilicia in Asia Minor (modern southwestern Turkey), where he executed his duties honorably, restoring order, and even undertaking a brief but very successful military campaign against some warring hill-tribes. The political situation back in Rome had been deteriorating for several years. The triumvir Crassus had been killed on military campaign in Parthia in 53, and the relationship between the remaining triumvirs, Caesar and Pompey, was fast approaching a breaking point.

Only a few weeks following Cicero's return to Rome from his governorship in Cilicia, full-scale civil war broke out (January, 49 BC). After much hesitation, personal deliberation, and a failed attempt to reconcile Caesar and Pompey, Cicero eventually joined the republican forces under the command of Pompey in Greece. But following their defeat at Pharsalus in 48, he returned to Italy and, after another stretch of agonizing uncertainty, was among those pardoned by Caesar and permitted to remain in the country; others in the republican cause, including Cato the Younger, fought on.

During the ensuing dictatorship of Caesar, Cicero again saw his opportunities for playing a significant role in the public arena greatly curtailed. Moreover, the tragic death of his beloved daughter, Tullia, in 45 BC forced him further into withdrawal and near despair. As he had done a decade earlier in forced retirement, he turned to writing as he searched for consolation, and during this period composed a remarkable number of rhetorical and philosophical works, including *Brutus*, *Orator*, *De finibus bonorum et malorum (On Moral Ends)*, *Tusculan Disputations*, and *De natura deorum (On the Nature of the Gods)*.

While not directly involved in the assassination of Julius Caesar on the Ides (15th) of March, 44 BC, Cicero viewed it as an opportunity for the Republic to rise again from its ashes. But the subsequent actions of Mark Antony, one of Caesar's close friends and his colleague in the consulship that year, soon led Cicero to fear that Rome had merely substituted one tyrant for another. Taking up what would be his final and perhaps most courageous cause, he managed to rally the people and the Senate of Rome through a series of speeches that he called *Philippics*, likening them by their title to the speeches that the great Greek orator Demosthenes had delivered three hundred years earlier against Philip II of Macedon. But in the end, Cicero's hopes of a restored Republic were dashed, when the young and ambitious grand-nephew and heir of Caesar, Octavian (later to be Caesar Augustus), joined forces with Antony and Marcus Aemilius Lepidus in a "Second Triumvirate," that immediately set about eliminating their opposition to control of the state. Cicero's name appeared prominently on the list of the proscribed, and after being hunted down near Formiae, his head and hands were severed from his body by Antony's minions and brought back to Rome, where they were prominently displayed on the rostra, the speakers' platform, where Cicero had so often stood to address the Roman people.

Cicero's enduring legacy stems largely from his writings. In fact, we know more about Cicero than perhaps any other person of antiquity, largely owing to the vast corpus of his works that survive today. Nearly sixty of his speeches are extant, as well as a score of philosophical and rhetorical works, and almost a thousand personal letters. These writings have been valued from his day down to our own times, and provide for us the portrait of the man in all of his dimensions—orator, rhetorician, politician, philosopher, and patriot.

HOW TO WIN AN ARGUMENT

THE ORIGINS OF ELOQUENT AND PERSUASIVE SPEECH

Nature, Art, Practice

The precise nature of eloquent and persuasive speech was fiercely debated in antiquity. Is rhetoric an actual art, or merely a skill, a knack? Does it require natural ability, or can it be mastered merely through the acquisition of certain techniques and the memorization of a body of rules and precepts? Generally, the ancient theorists spoke of a requisite triad: natural ability or inborn talent, mastery of the art of speaking as outlined in rhetorical treatises (called artes *in Latin), and diligent application of one's talent and training through practice. In his earliest published work,* De inventione, *or* On Invention, *written when he was about 17 years old, Cicero offers an explanation of the origin of eloquence.*

And if we wish to consider the origin of this thing that is called eloquence—whether it be an art or a study or some sort of skill or a faculty bestowed by nature—we will discover that it was born from most honorable causes and continued its development for the best of reasons. For there was a time when people wandered in the fields far and wide, like beasts, and preserved their existence relying on uncultivated food; no rational system of religion or of societal obligation was yet practiced; no one had witnessed legitimate marriage, nor had anyone looked upon children whom he knew for certain to be his own, nor had they realized what advantages an equitable code of law might provide. So, because of their own error and ignorance, a blind and reckless passion controlled them, and, in order to satisfy itself, continually misused bodily strength, the most dangerous of servants.

At this point in time, a man—great and wise to be sure—came to recognize the innate potential and the boundless opportunity for great accomplishments residing in the human spirit, if only someone could draw it out and improve it through instruction. He systematically assembled the people in one place; scattered in the fields and living hidden in their woodland shelters, he brought them together, introducing them to every useful and honorable pursuit. At first, because of the novelty of the thing, they strongly objected; but then, as they began to listen more earnestly, he transformed them through reason and speech from wild, savage creatures into tame and gentle people.

To me, at least, it does not seem possible that mute wisdom, devoid of speaking ability, was suddenly able to turn people from their accustomed ways and lead them to different modes of living. What is more, once cities had been established, how could it have happened that people learned to honor faith and uphold justice, and became accustomed to obeying others willingly, and judged that they must not only take on great tasks for the sake of the common good but even sacrifice their lives, unless others had been able to persuade them by eloquence of those things that they had discovered by reason? Certainly, no one who was endowed with great physical strength would have willingly and without violence submitted himself to the law, allowing himself to be put on an equal footing with those over whom he could excel, abandoning voluntarily a most agreeable custom—especially a custom that had through the course of time already acquired the force of a law of nature—, had he not been moved by speech both powerful and persuasive.

Eloquence, then, seems initially to have originated in this way, and to have advanced to greater development, and likewise subsequently, in the most important matters of peace and war, to have been involved with the highest interests of humankind. (*De inventione* 1.2–3)

Some 30 years later, Cicero wrote De oratore (On the Ideal Orator), *a masterful treatise in which he constructs a portrait of his ideal speaker. The work is composed as a dialogue between several of the leading orators of the generation previous to Cicero's; the two main characters of the dialogue are Lucius Crassus and Marcus Antonius, Cicero's boyhood mentors and the greatest orators of Rome at that time. In the following passage, the interlocutor Crassus refers to these same origins of eloquence; he extols the capacity for speech as one of the most powerful and efficacious of all human gifts, and encourages his young protégés to master the art of eloquence:*

Actually, I think nothing is more admirable than being able, through speech, to take hold of human minds, to win over their inclinations, to drive them at will in one direction, and to draw them at will from another. It is this ability, more than anything else, that has ever flourished, ever reigned supreme in every free nation and especially in quiet and peaceful communities. What could be so wonderful as when out of an infinite crowd one human being emerges who—alone or with very few others—is able to use with effect the faculty that is a natural gift to all? Or what is so pleasing to the mind and to the ear as speech distinguished and refined by wise thoughts and impressive words? Or what so powerful and so splendid as one man's speech transforming the impulses of the people, the scruples of jurors, or the authority of the Senate? Again, what is so regal, so generous, so magnanimous, as lending aid to those in distress, raising up the afflicted, offering people safety, freeing them from dangers, saving them from exile? At the same time, what is so vital as always having the weapons available with which you can shield yourself and challenge the wicked or take revenge when attacked? But really, let us not always be preoccupied with the forum, with the court-benches, the rostra, and the Senate House: if we consider our leisure time, what can be more pleasant or more properly human than to be able to engage in elegant conversation and show oneself a stranger to no subject? For the one thing that most especially sets us above animals is that we converse with one another, and that we can express our thoughts through speech. Who, then, would not rightly admire this ability, and would not think that he should take the greatest pains in order to surpass other human beings in the very thing that especially makes humans themselves superior to beasts? But let us now turn to what is surely the most important point of all: what other force could have gathered the scattered members of the human race into one place, or could have led them away from a savage existence in the wilderness to this truly human, communal way of life, or, once communities had been founded, could have established laws, judicial procedures, and civic rights? And to avoid enumerating still more points (they are actually almost numberless), let me summarize everything in a few words: I assert that the leadership and wisdom of the perfect orator provide the chief basis, not only for his own dignity, but also for the safety of countless individuals and of the State at large. Therefore, young men, continue your present efforts and devote all your energies to the pursuit you are following, so that you can bring honor to yourselves, service to your friends, and benefit to the State. (*De oratore* 1.30–34)

Cicero, while obviously keenly aware and knowledgeable of the rules contained in the typical rhetorical treatises of his day, was highly critical of mere "handbook learning." In fact, in De oratore *(On the Ideal Orator), he routinely criticizes the hackneyed precepts of the handbooks. They perhaps serve a foundational purpose, but the ideal orator must, in addition to knowledge of rhetorical rules, possess a vast knowledge of all the humane arts, including history, literature, law, and philosophy (see later, 126–134). Such knowledge, along with natural ability, study, and diligent practice are essential for winning an argument.*

. . . there exists a kind of observation of what is effective in speaking; but if this could make people eloquent, then everybody would be eloquent. For who would not be able to master this easily, or at least in some way or other? But in my view, such rules are powerful and useful, not because art can lead us to discover what to say, but because, when we have learned a proper point of reference, rules may assure us of the soundness, or make us see the weakness, of whatever we accomplish by means of our own natural ability, our study, and our training. (*De oratore* 2.232)

Rhetoric and Truth

The power wielded by a skillful speaker, who knows how to persuade through artful speech and appeal to human emotions, is, as outlined earlier, a powerful weapon. It is, in fact, a two-edged sword, one that can be employed for good or for ill. We need only to consider two extraordinarily effective twentieth-century orators who were embroiled in the same conflict, Winston Churchill and Adolf Hitler, to illustrate this point graphically. In such a context, it is easy to see why the word "rhetoric" often carries with it today a negative connotation. In ancient Greece, after the creation of a rhetorical system that was based largely on the principle of argumentation founded on probability, teachers of rhetoric emerged who rejected the ideal sphere of pure reason and absolute truth in favor of the probable and relative, who extolled the power of the word, and who sometimes endeavored to make the worse seem the better cause. Philosophers like Socrates and Plato, on the contrary, searching for final and absolute ends, championed truth uncovered through dialectical inquiry. Thus, the so-called quarrel between rhetoric and philosophy emerged, a quarrel that would endure, in varying manifestations and in varying levels of intensity, down to Cicero's time. The opening paragraph of Cicero's De inventione *(On Invention) reveals his thoughts on the matter:*

Often and much have I pondered the question of whether fluency of speech and a consuming devotion to eloquence have brought more good or evil to people and their communities. For when I consider the injuries done to our Republic, and review in my mind the ancient calamities of prominent communities, I see that no little part of their misfortunes was brought about through the agency of men who were highly skilled in speaking. On the other hand, when I set out on a search in the annals of literature for events that, because of their antiquity, are removed from our generation's memory, I find that many cities have been founded, the flames of very many wars have been extinguished, the firmest alliances and the most hallowed friendships have been formed not only by the mind's power of reason but also more easily by eloquence. And after reflecting on it for a long time, that same power of reason leads me to form this opinion first and foremost: wisdom without eloquence does too little for the good of communities, but eloquence without wisdom is, in most instances, extremely harmful and never beneficial. If, then, anyone exerts all of his energies in the practice of oratory to the neglect of the highest and most honorable pursuits of reason and moral conduct, he is reared as a citizen useless to himself and harmful to his country; but the person who arms himself with eloquence in such a way that enables him not to assail the interests of his country, but rather assist them, this man, in my opinion, will be a citizen most helpful and most devoted both to his own interests and those of the public. (Cicero, *De Inventione* I. 1)

Several decades later, in his De oratore, *Cicero will speak in more detail concerning the quarrel*

*and will strive to effect a reconciliation or syn-
thesis, combining philosophy, not so much with
rhetoric, but with eloquence. Cicero's ideal orator is an oratorical philosopher, or a philosophical
orator. Nonetheless, it is clear to anyone familiar
with Cicero's oratorical career that on several occasions he defended clients whom he knew to be
guilty. In fact, a later teacher of rhetoric, Quintilian, reports to us that Cicero once boasted that,
in his defense of a client named Cluentius, he
"threw dust in the eyes of the jury." Addressing
his son near the end of his life, Cicero has something to say about defending guilty clients; it appears that our notion of granting every defendant a fair trial has at least some of its foundation
in Cicero's way of thinking:*

And this precept of moral duty must be assiduously maintained: never lodge in court a capital
charge against an innocent person; indeed, there
is no way this can be done without making oneself a criminal. For what is more inhuman than
to turn one's eloquence, a gift bestowed by nature for the safety and preservation of our fellow humans, to the destruction and ruin of good
people? Nevertheless, while this practice must

be avoided, we need not be overly scrupulous about defending a guilty person, provided he is not abominably wicked—people want this; custom sanctions it; humanity accepts it. In court cases, it is always the duty of the juror to pursue the truth; it is sometimes the duty of the advocate to defend what is similar to the truth, even if it be less than the truth. (*De officiis* 2.51)

THE PARTS OF RHETORIC, OR ACTIVITIES OF THE ORATOR

Those who in antiquity taught and wrote about the art of persuasion regularly identified three genres of oratory, or types of cases: "judicial," suited to seeking justice in courts of law; "deliberative," whose goal is to argue what is most beneficial or expedient in a public meeting or before an assembly; and "epideictic" or "demonstrative," the oratory of praise or blame, perhaps best illustrated by the funeral oration or eulogy. Handbooks tended to concentrate on the judicial genre, as perhaps being most crucial and as lending itself best to systematic exposition. Ancient theorists organized their presentation around five parts, or activities of the orator: "invention" (discovering, that is, thinking out the material), "arrangement" (ordering the material), "style" (putting the ordered material into appropriate words), "memory" (memorizing the speech), and "delivery" (including directives about voice, facial expression, and gesture). These parts or activities parallel the process through which a speaker proceeds when composing and delivering a speech. Instruction in English composition, even in modern times, continued to endorse this process, at least through the first three stages; those composing a speech or a detailed argument today will still find these activities effective means for organizing and presenting their points.

Invention: Identifying and Classifying the Question at Issue According to the Stance of Argument, and Discovering the Sources of Proof

Invention (Latin invention) *is concerned with finding and thinking out the subject matter of the speech; the process chiefly involves identifying and classifying the question at issue according to a specific stance of argument, as well as discovering the most promising sources of proof for persuading one's audience.*

Status *(Stances of Argument)*

In a judicial controversy, the charge of the prosecution and the counter-claim by the defense crystallize the question at issue, that is, the matter under judgment, which in turn is classified according to one of four "stances of argument" (Latin status *or* constitutio*), that is, according to the stand that is assumed by the defense. Cicero succinctly outlines this system in* De inventione *1.10:*

Every subject that contains in itself some controversy situated in speech and debate involves a question about a fact, or about a definition, or about the nature or quality of an act, or about legal processes. Therefore, we call the question from which the whole case arises the *status*, or "issue." The "issue" is the first conflict of pleas that arises from the defense of the accusation, in this manner: "You did it"; "I did not do it," or "I was justified in doing it." When the dispute is about a fact, the issue is called "conjectural," because the plea is supported by conjectures or inferences [for example, "you did it"; "I did not"]. When, however, the issue is about a definition, it is called the "definitional" issue, because the meaning of the term must be defined in words [for example, "you did it"; "yes, but it wasn't theft"]. When the nature or quality of the act is examined, the issue is called "qualitative," inasmuch as the controversy concerns the value of the action and its class or quality [for example, "you did it"; "yes, but I didn't mean to," or "I had to"]. But when the plea depends on the circumstance that it seems the right person does not bring the case, or that he brings it against the wrong person, or before the wrong court, or at the wrong time, under the wrong statute, or for the wrong charge, or with the wrong penalty, the issue is called "translative" because the actions appears to require a transfer to another court or a change in the form of pleading. One of these issues is necessarily applicable in every kind of case; for where none applies, there can be no controversy.

The Sources of Proof

Three hundred years before Cicero's time, the Greek philosopher Aristotle, in his handbook On Rhetoric, *identified two kinds of available means of persuasion for winning one's case or argument, what he called nonartistic and artistic proofs. Nonartistic proofs are those that the speaker does not invent by using his art, for example, written contracts and the testimony of witnesses; artistic means of persuasion, which the speaker does create by employing his art, are three in number:* logos *(rational argumentation),* ethos *(the presentation of character), and* pathos *(the arousal of emotions in the audience). Cicero adopts this Aristotelian schema, which we see reflected in the remarks made by Antonius, one of the chief characters of* De oratore, *as he describes his approach in handling the initial stage of invention:*

Well then, after accepting a case and acquainting myself with its category, the very first thing I do when I start working on the matter is to establish the point of reference for the whole portion of the speech that specifically concerns the judgment of the issue itself [that is, *status*]. After that, I consider very carefully two further elements: the first one recommends us or those for whom we are pleading, the second is aimed at moving the minds of our audience in the direction we want. The method employed in the art of oratory, then, relies entirely upon three means of persuasion: proving that our contentions are true [that is, *logos*], winning over our audience [that is, *ethos*], and inducing their minds to feel any emotion the case may demand [that is, *pathos*]. Now, for the purpose of proving, the orator has two kinds of material at his disposal. One consists of the things that are not thought out by the orator, but, inherent in the circumstances of the case, are treated methodically by him, such as documents, testimonies, agreements, evidence extracted by torture, laws, decrees of the Senate, judicial precedents, magistrates' rulings, legal opinions, and whatever else is not discovered by the orator, but is presented to him by the case and the parties involved. The other kind is that which entirely depends on the reasoning and argumentation of the orator. So in dealing with the first type, one must think about how to treat the arguments; with the second, about discovering them as well. (*De oratore* 2.114–17)

*The so-called artistic means of persuasion, that is, those that are thought out or created by the speaker, often employ "topics" or "commonplaces" (*loci communes *in Latin); these are "commonplace" or stereotypical logical strategies or premises* *(the latter often ethical or political) upon which a speaker can build his logical arguments or his appeals to character and emotion.*

This idea that I began weaving just now, resumed Antonius, was leading up to the following conclusion (seeing that it is understood that all issues called into question depend not on the innumerable individual persons or unlimited variety of occasions, but on cases of a general kind and on the character of the categories involved; and further, that these categories are not only restricted in number, but are even very few): those who are eagerly devoted to oratory should master the material belonging to each of the categories, marked, equipped with, and given distinction by all the commonplaces, that is, by subject matter and ideas. These by themselves will produce the words, which I, at any rate, always think sufficiently distinguished if they are such that the subject matter itself seems to have produced them. And if you want to know the truth, at least as I see it (for I can affirm nothing but my own view and opinion on the matter), we ought to bring this equipment of general, abstract cases with us into the forum; we should not be searching the commonplaces from which arguments can be unearthed only at the moment that a case has been entrusted to us. For surely everyone who has given them only moderate consideration can come to know such arguments in every detail through application and experience. At the same time, our minds must be directed back to those sources and to those commonplaces, as I have already called them, from which everything that can be discovered and invented for any speech is derived. In fact, the whole thing boils down to this (whether it is a matter of art or observation or experience): knowing the areas where you must hunt for, and track down, what you are trying to find. Once you have surrounded the entire place with the nets of your thought, at least if practical experience has sharpened your skill, nothing will escape you, and everything that is in the subject matter will run up to you and fall into your hands. (*De oratore* 2. 145–47)

LOGOS (RATIONAL ARGUMENTATION)

Rational argumentation has its foundation in two basic processes, induction and deduction. Speakers today still rely on these weapons of logic to win an argument, employing induction by the use of example and deduction through syllogistic reasoning.

Examples, or analogies, can be fictitious or historical, and from them you can argue by inducing a probable conclusion about the matter in dispute, and then offer a general or universal application drawn from the specific example in question. Such arguments generally are tripartite in nature, first presenting one or more similar cases, second stating the point we want conceded, for which the similar cases have been cited, and third drawing a conclusion that reinforces the concession or demonstrates what results follow from it.

A syllogism has the basic form of major premise, minor premise, and conclusion, for example, "All human beings are mortal; Cicero is a human being; therefore, Cicero is mortal." In speeches and oral arguments, a speaker often relies on premises that are probable and not necessarily certain, and sometimes even omits the minor premise, thus expressing the earlier syllogism in this way: "Cicero is mortal, because all humans are." This sort of "rhetorical syllogism" is known as an enthymeme. In its most expansive, five-part form, called the epicheireme, a syllogism's major *and minor premises are supported by further arguments, and then the conclusion is drawn.*

An entertaining argument demonstrating induction (that is, use of example or analogy) is related by Cicero in De Inventione *(1.51–52):*

In the writings of Aeschines Socraticus, Socrates lays out an argument presented to Xenophon and his wife by Aspasia: "Please tell me, madam Xenophon, if your neighbor should have finer gold jewelry than you have, would you prefer hers or your own?" "Hers," she replied. "What if she should have clothing and other feminine accessories that are more expensive than what you have—would you prefer yours or hers?" "Hers, of course," she responded. "Well, then, what if she should have a better husband than you have—would you prefer yours or hers?" At this the woman blushed. Then Aspasia initiated a conversation with Xenophon himself. "Please tell me, Xenophon, if your neighbor should have a better horse than yours, which would you prefer, yours or his?" "His," he replied. "What if he had a better farm than yours—which farm would you prefer to have?" "The better farm, to be sure," he answered. "Now, what if he should have a better wife than you have—would you prefer his or yours?" At this, Xenophon also fell silent. Then Aspasia said, "Since each of you did not answer the one and only question to which I wanted an answer, I will tell you what each of you is thinking. You, wife, want to have the best husband, and you, Xenophon, want above all to have the finest wife. If, therefore, you cannot arrange it so that there be no better husband or finer wife on earth, you will surely be seeking eagerly what you think best, namely, that you be married to the best possible wife, and that she be wedded to the best possible husband." Here, since assent has been granted to statements that are undisputed, even the point that would seem in doubt when asked by itself is, by analogy, conceded as certain, because of the method employed in putting the question.

*In the following passage (*De inventione *1.58–59), Cicero illustrates deductive reasoning in his outline of the* epicheireme, *the expansive, five-part syllogism. Note, however, that in proving the major premise here, induction (that is, the use of example) is also employed:*

Those who think a syllogism should be argued in five parts say that the first part should state the thesis of the argument in this manner: "Things that are done by design are managed better than those that are administered without design." They number this as the first part; and they believe that it should be substantiated by a variety of reasons and with great copiousness of expression, in this way: "The household that is managed by careful planning is in all respects better equipped and better prepared than the one that is governed by chance and without a plan. The army that is commanded by a wise and skillful general is in all respects guided more advantageously than the one administered by someone's folly and rashness. The same reasoning can be applied to navigation; for the ship that employs the most knowledgeable helmsman completes its voyage most successfully." When the proposition has been proved in this way and two parts of the syllogism have been completed, they say that you should in the third part [that is, the minor premise] state what you want to demonstrate, issuing from the thought of the major premise, in this manner: "Of all things nothing is better governed than the universe." In the fourth part, they adduce another proof in support of this premise: "For the risings and the settings of the constellations preserve a definite order and the seasonal changes of the year not only occur necessarily always in the same way, but also agreeably to the advantage of all nature; and the alteration of day and night has through its changes in no respect ever harmed anything." These points are all proof that the nature of the universe is governed by some sort of extraordinary plan. In the fifth place, they draw the conclusion, which either merely states the inevitable deduction from all the parts, in this manner: "Therefore the universe is administered by design"; or after briefly joining together the major and minor premises in one statement, they add what follows from them, in this way: "Therefore if those things that are governed by design are administered better than those that are governed without design, and of all things nothing is governed better than the universe, then the universe is governed by design." The five-part argument, according to their thought, is structured in this way.

ETHOS (ARGUMENT BASED ON CHARACTER)

The second mode or source of proof is ethos, *or "character," that is, persuasion gained through*

*the effective presentation of the speaker's char-
acter or the character of the person on whose behalf the speaker is pleading. The goal is to win
the approval and admiration of your audience,
which makes them ultimately more sympathetic
to your argument. Negative character portrayal
of your opponent is also an effective way to help
your listeners side with your point of view. In this
passage from* De oratore (On the Ideal Orator)
(2.182–84), *Cicero expounds on the effectiveness
of persuasion achieved through character portrayal:*

Well then, the character, the customs, the deeds,
and the life, both of those who do the pleading and
of those on whose behalf they plead, make a very
important contribution to winning a case. These
should be approved of, and the corresponding
elements in the opponents should meet with disapproval, and the minds of the audience should,
as much as possible, be won over to feel goodwill
toward the orator as well as toward his client.
Now people's minds are won over by a man's
prestige, his accomplishments, and the reputation he has acquired by his way of life. Such
things are easier to embellish if present than to

fabricate if totally lacking, but at any rate, their effect is enhanced by a gentle tone of voice on the part of the orator, an expression on his face intimating restraint, and kindliness in the use of his words, and if you press some point rather vigorously, by seeming to act against your inclination, because you are forced to do so. Indications of flexibility, on the part of the orator and the client, are also quite useful, as well as signs of generosity, mildness, dutifulness, gratitude, and of not being desirous or greedy. Actually, all qualities typical of people who are decent and unassuming, not severe, not obstinate, not litigious, not harsh, really win goodwill, and alienate the audience from those who do not possess them. And these same considerations must likewise be employed to ascribe the opposite qualities to our opponents. But this entire mode of speaking is most effective in cases where there is not much opportunity to use some form of sharp and violent emotional arousal to set the juror's heart aflame. For we don't always have to employ vigorous oratory, but often we should rather speak in a quiet, low-keyed, and gentle manner. This is particularly effective in recommending parties to the audience. (By "parties" I mean not only those who are accused, but all those whose interests are at stake—for this is how the word was used in the old days.) Portraying their characters in your speech, then, as being just, upright, conscientious toward the gods, subject to fear, and patient of injustice, is enormously influential. And if this is handled agreeably and with taste, it is actually so powerful—whether done in the prologue or when narrating the facts or when bringing the speech to its conclusion—that it often has more influence than the case itself. Moreover, so much is accomplished by speaking thoughtfully and with a certain taste, that the speech may be said to mold an image of the character of the orator. Employing thoughts of a certain kind and words of a certain kind, and adopting besides a delivery that is gentle and shows signs of flexibility, makes speakers appear as decent, as good in character— yes, as good men.

In most cases, ethical persuasion is presented subtly and throughout a speech (Cicero likens it to blood flowing through the entire body), and by the end of the speech or argument a particular portrait has been drawn for the hearers, both of the speaker and his opponent, and often others who have something to do with the argument or case in question. For example, in his defense of Roscius of Ameria (in 80 BC), who was charged with the heinous crime of murdering his own father, Cicero repeatedly and consistently portrays his client as a simple, frugal farmer whose character could never entertain the thought of a crime as atrocious as parricide; Roscius's adversaries, on the other hand, corrupted by their prodigality and prodded by their greed and audacity, are capable of any outrage, as he points out in this short passage from the middle of his speech:

In this regard, I pass over what could have been an extremely powerful argument for me in maintaining Roscius's innocence—the fact that crimes of this sort are not generally born amid rustic manners, a frugal mode of living, a life rough and uncultured. Just as you cannot find every sort of crop or tree growing in every sort of soil, so every kind of life does not give birth to every kind of crime. The city breeds prodigality, and from prodigality greed necessarily develops, and from greed audacity bursts forth, from which all crimes and evil deeds are born.

On the other hand, this rustic sort of life, which you call countrified, is the teacher of thriftiness, diligence, and justice. (*Pro Roscio Amerino 75*)

A much more blatant use of character-based proof is evident in a speech from the time of Cicero's consulship in 63 BC. Toward the end of his year in office, Cicero uncovered a plot to overthrow the government, masterminded by Catiline, a nobly born but overly ambitious and unscrupulous senator, who had actually been one of Cicero's fellow-competitors for the consulship in the previous year. After denouncing Catiline in a meeting of the Senate, Cicero spoke to the Roman people in public assembly, presenting them with the facts surrounding the conspiracy. In this speech, he makes blatant and unrestrained use of arguments based on character as he endeavors to draw a sharp comparison between himself and the loyal citizens of Rome and Catiline and his morally bankrupt followers. As is readily evident in this passage (In Catilinam 2.22–25), no subtlety is at play here, but something more akin to character assassination. Incidentally, it is worth noting that ad hominem *attacks and proof based on character, which more often than not are excluded from our courtrooms, were not only permitted but even expected in the Roman setting.*

The final group is not only last in order but also in character and way of life—Catiline's own, of his own choosing, or rather sprung from his most intimate embrace. You see them with carefully coiffured hair, glistening with oil, some clean-shaven, others well-bearded, wearing ankle-and-wrist-length tunics, wrapped in togas that look more like sails. They drain all their life's energy and all the work of their waking hours in banquets that last until dawn. In these herds, you'll see all the gamblers, all the adulterers, all the dirty and disgusting lechers. These boys, so sleek and dainty, have learned not only to love and to be loved, not only to dance and sing, but even to brandish daggers and pour poison. If they do not leave Rome, if they do not perish, even if Catiline perishes, know that a breeding ground of Catilines will abide in the Republic. And yet, what do such wretches want for themselves? They are not going to bring their little girlfriends into camp with them, are they? But how will they be able to live without them, especially on nights like these? How will they endure the frost and snow of the Apennines? Unless, of course, they believe they will endure winter more easily because they have previously learned to dance at banquets in the nude.

What an extraordinarily terrifying war it will be if Catiline will be leading this praetorian cohort of whores! Now, citizens, draw up your garrisons and armies against these outstanding troops of Catiline! First, post your consuls and generals against that wounded and worn-out gladiator; next, lead out the flower and strength of all of Italy against that castaway, debilitated band of shipwrecked men. . . . I have no need to compare your other resources, your equipment, your garrisons, with the poverty and neediness of that bandit. But if, leaving aside all of those things with which we are supplied and that man lacks—namely the Senate, the equestrian order, the city of Rome, the treasury, tax revenue, all of Italy, all of the provinces, if leaving aside all of these considerations, we are willing to compare the two causes that are in conflict, from this comparison alone we can understand how utterly prostrate our enemies lie. On our side fights modesty, on their side impudence; on our side decency, on theirs disgracefulness; on our side good faith, on theirs deceit; on ours dutifulness, on theirs criminality; on ours firmness of purpose, on theirs raving madness; on ours the honorable, on theirs the base; on ours continency, on theirs lust; finally, justice, temperance, fortitude, prudence—all the virtues contend with injustice, prodigality, cowardice, imprudence—with all the vices. In sum, abundance fights against poverty, propriety against profligacy, sanity against madness, and well-founded hope against desperation in all things. In a contest and battle of this sort, even if men's enthusiasm should flag, would not the immortal gods themselves compel such a multitude of egregious vices to submit to these most outstanding virtues?

PATHOS (ARGUMENT BASED ON EMOTIONAL APPEAL)

The third source of proof is pathos, *or persuasion won through appeal to the audience's emotions. The speaker's goal is to sway, or move (*movere *in Latin) the feelings of his listeners so that they will side emotionally with him. Appealing to the emotions is a tactic as old as speech itself, and the Greeks and the Romans employed both verbal and nonverbal appeals. One might recall that Socrates, in his defense called the* Apology, *as-*

serted that he would not resort to emotional appeals, for example, bringing his children into the courtroom, dressed in mourning clothes, to secure his acquittal. Cicero realized the great power of argument based on emotional appeal, often calling it the most effective means of persuasion. For him, ethos *involved knowledge and exploitation of the milder emotions, while* pathos *dealt with the more violent emotions. In* De oratore *(2.185– 87), the interlocutor Antonius continues with his description of* pathos:

Related to this [that is, *ethos*], though of a different order, is the other mode of speaking I mentioned, which stirs the hearts of the jurors quite differently, impelling them to hate or to love, to envy someone or to want his safety, to fear or to hope, to feel favor or aversion, to feel joy or grief, to pity or to want punishment, or to be led to whatever feelings are near and akin to those other such emotions. Of course, the most desirable situation for the orator is when the jurors themselves come to the case in an emotional state of mind, suited to what his own interests demand. For, as the saying goes, it is easier to spur on a willing horse than to rouse a sluggish one. But if this is not the case, or if the situation is rather unclear, then my method is that of a diligent doctor: before attempting to apply treatment to a patient, he must find out, not only about the disease of the person he wants to cure, but also about his routine when healthy and his physical constitution. I do likewise myself: when I set out to work upon the emotions of the jurors in a difficult and uncertain case, I carefully concentrate all of my thoughts on considering, on scenting out as keenly as I can, what their feelings, their opinions, their hopes, and their wishes are, and in what direction my speech may most easily lead them. If they put themselves into my hands and, as I just said, are inclined, of their own accord, to lean in the direction I am pushing them, I accept what is offered and spread my sails to catch any breeze that happens to be blowing. If, however, the jurors are unbiased and unemotional, more effort is required; for then, the given situation offers no help, and all feelings must be stirred by my speech alone. But such enormous power is wielded by what one of our good poets rightly describes as "soul-bending, the queen of all the world—speech," that it cannot only straighten up someone who is bending over and bend over someone who is standing, but also, like a good and brave general, take prisoner someone who is offering resistance and fighting back.

Antonius next goes on to assert that, in order to be most effective in stirring the emotions, the speaker himself should actually feel those emotions he hopes to evoke. He then describes his own appeal to pathos *in one of the more famous examples of such pyrotechnics:*

Do not imagine that I didn't feel enormous grief in doing what I did when concluding my speech for Manius Aquillius, when I had to preserve his status as a citizen. For I remembered him to have been consul, to have been general, that he had been honored by the Senate, and had climbed the Capitol in celebration of his *ovatio*. So, when I saw him crushed, weakened, mourning, brought to the brink of disaster, I did not attempt to arouse pity in others before having been overwhelmed with pity myself. I clearly sensed that the jurors were especially moved at the point when I called forward the grieving old man, dressed in mourning clothes, and when I was prompted not by rhetorical theory (I wouldn't know what to say about that), but by my deep grief and passion, to do what you, Crassus, were praising—I ripped open his tunic and exposed his scars [that is, scars he had sustained fighting on behalf of the state]. Gaius Marius, who was present at the trial among his supporters, strongly heightened the sorrow of my speech with his tears, and I, repeatedly addressing him, commended his colleague to his protection, and appealed to him to stand in defense of the common interests of generals. When I uttered these lamentations, and also had invoked all gods and men, all citizens and allies, it was not without shedding tears and feeling enormous grief myself. If there had been no grief in all of the words that I delivered on that occasion, my speech, so far from stirring pity, would actually have been ridiculous. (*De oratore* 2.194–96)

Cicero was well-known for his effective use of pathos *in his own speeches, often employing the grand style, full of emotion, to sway the jury in his client's favor. In the following passage, taken from the conclusion, or peroration, of his defense of his friend Plancius, Cicero pulls out all the emotional stops to secure the acquittal of his client, who was on trial for illegal election activities. A few years before the trial, when Plancius was stationed in Thessalonica, he offered shelter and support to Cicero, who had been exiled from Rome, a victim of the machinations of his archenemy Clodius. Throughout the speech, and especially here at its end, Cicero makes allusion to Plancius's aid to him in his hour of darkness, and links Plancius's current plight with his own situation while in exile.*

Oh, those watches of yours, Plancius, so wretched! Oh, those vigils full of tears! Oh, those bitter nights! Oh, that calamitous care for my life—if you, whom I could have aided perhaps by my death, cannot now receive help from me while I am alive! I remember, indeed I remember—nor shall I ever forget—that night when, in my misery, led on by false hope, I made empty, vain promises to you, as you sat by my side, watching and grieving with me: that I, if I were ever restored to my country, would repay your present kindness; but if fate should snatch life from me, or if some other force beyond my control should prevent my return, I promised that these, these men (for who else at that time was in my thoughts) would pay full recompense to you for all of your labors on my behalf. Why are you looking at me in that way? Why are you claiming my promises? Why are you imploring my good faith? I promised nothing to you then that was dependent upon my own resources; rather I made promises, relying on the benevolence of these men toward me; I knew that they were mourning for me, sighing for me, willing to fight for my life, even at peril to their own lives. When I was with you, I heard reports daily about their yearning, their sorrow, their laments; and now I fear that I can repay to you nothing beyond the tears you shed so bounteously for me amid my calamities. For what else can I do but grieve, but weep, but bind you by embrace to my own salvation? For the same people who granted salvation to me are able to grant it to you. But you—stand up, I beg—you I will hold and embrace: I profess myself to be not only an intercessor on behalf of your fortunes, but also your partner and ally. And there will be no one, I hope, so hard-hearted and inhuman, no one so forgetful, I will not say of my services to the patriots, but of their services to me, as to pull or tear from my side the savior of my person. I plead to you, jurors, not on behalf of one who has benefited from my services, but for one who was the guardian of my welfare; my weapons are not wealth, not authority, not influence, but prayers, tears, pity. And with me, this most excellent but wretched parent implores you, and we two fathers plead on behalf of one son. By you and your fortunes, by your children, I beg that you not willingly provide a source of joy to my enemies, especially those whom I incurred on behalf of your welfare, allowing them to boast that you, now forgetful of my welfare, stand as enemies of the man by whom that welfare was preserved. Do not shatter my spirit now with grief, and then again with the fear that your goodwill toward me has changed; allow me from your store of graciousness to fulfill the promise that I, relying on you, often made to my client. Gaius Flavius, I beg and implore you earnestly—you who during my consulship were an ally of my plans, who shared in my dangers and helped with what I accomplished, and who always has wished not only for my safety, but for my honor and success—to do me the favor of saving, through the agency of this jury, the man through whose agency I, as you know, was saved to serve you and them. Your tears, and yours, jurors, not to mention my own, prevent me from saying more — tears that, in the midst of my great fear, suddenly give me hope that you will display the same disposition in saving my client as you did in saving me; for seeing your tears now calls to my mind those tears that you so often and so profusely have shed for me. (*Pro Plancio* 101–4)

Arrangement

Arrangement is the second part of rhetoric, or the second activity of the speaker. Now equipped with the subject matter for your argument or speech — having determined the issue at hand, thought out appropriate supporting arguments drawn from the sources of proof, and identified commonplaces through which to present these arguments — it is time to arrange or organize your speech appropriately into parts. By most accounts, a judicial speech in its basic form has four parts, an introduction or prologue, a narration or statement of the case, an argument including a refutation of opposing arguments, and a conclusion or epilogue. Deliberative speeches may sometimes assume a different structure. Moreover, at times a speaker might find it appropriate to add a proposition, a statement or division of his arguments, or a digression, an excursus on some related facet of the case, often on the character or actions of one of the principles involved. In De oratore *2.307–12, Cicero's interlocutor Antonius responds to an earlier comment from his friend, Catulus, and gives advice on the arrangement of material:*

So let me now return to the subject that earned me your praise a little while ago, Catulus, the order and the arrangement of the material and the commonplaces. The principles involved are two; one is inherent in the nature of our cases, the other is a matter of the judgment and good sense of the speaker. That we should say something before addressing the case, then set forth the case, after that prove it by establishing our own arguments and refuting those of our opponents, then conclude our speech and so bring it to an end—this is prescribed by the very nature of oratory. But to determine how we are to put together what we have to say in order to give proof and to instruct the jurors—that is the special province of the orator's good sense. For there are always many arguments that occur to us, many that seem likely to bring us advantage in our speech. Some of these, however, carry so little weight that they must be disregarded. Others, even if they offer some help, are often such that they contain some fault, while the value of the advantage that they seem to provide is not so great that it should be combined with some harmful point. But as to the useful and strong arguments, if nevertheless a great number of them remain, as often happens, then those among them that carry the least weight, or are rather similar to other, weightier ones, ought to be discarded, I think, and to be removed from our speech. It is at least my own practice, when I am assembling arguments for my cases, not to count so much as to weigh them.

Also, as I have often said already, we bring people over to our point of view in three ways, either by instructing them [that is, *logos*] or by winning their goodwill [that is, *ethos*] or by stirring their emotions [that is, *pathos*]. Well, one of these methods we should openly display, and we must appear to aim at nothing but giving instruction, while the other two must, just like blood in the body, flow throughout the whole of the speech. For it is essential that not only the prologues but also the other parts of a speech, about which I shall presently say a few words, should have the power to seep into the minds of the audience. As regards those two elements of a speech (which, though they do not provide instruction by argument, still accomplish a great deal by persuading and moving), it is true that both the introduction and the end of a speech are especially appropriate places for them; nevertheless, it is often useful to digress from the proposition you are arguing in order to stir the emotions. Accordingly, after the case has been set forth in the narration, there is often room for inserting a digression aimed at stirring the emotions. Or this may well be done after our arguments have been proven or after those of our opponents have been refuted, or in both places, or in all parts of the speech, if there is enough importance and substance to the case. Actually, the cases that can best be amplified and given distinction, being weightiest and fullest, are exactly those that offer the most starting points for digressions of the kind that allow us to employ the commonplaces that drive on or deflect the audience's emotional impulses.

Introduction or Prologue
(Latin Exordium)

The exordium, *or prologue, of the speech is a passage designed to bring our audience into the proper state of mind in order to receive the rest of our argument. To accomplish this goal, the speaker should strive to secure the attention of his listeners, to make them receptive and ready to receive his arguments, and to win their goodwill. Ancient handbooks generally contain detailed descriptions of tactics that are effective in meeting these goals. Cicero's earliest extant oration (*Pro Quinctio, On Behalf of Quinctius*) *offers a fine example of an* exordium, *one particularly aimed at securing the sympathy and goodwill of his listeners, while at the same time disposing them unfavorably toward his opponents. The case is a relatively complicated one, involving a dispute over property possession. In his introduction, Cicero draws effective character sketches [that is,* ethos] *of those involved in the case: Naevius, the powerful and unscrupulous adversary; Hortensius, his patron, the eloquent and well-established orator; Quinctius, the poor, downtrodden defendant; and Cicero himself, Quinctius's patron, who is work-*

ing at a great disadvantage, and whose abilities and experience pale in comparison to those of his opponent. In addition, Cicero's characterization of and appeal to Gaius Aquilius, chief assessor in the case, demonstrate his rather blatant efforts at securing the goodwill of his audience for the remainder of his speech:

Two things that wield extraordinary power in the state—I mean great influence and eloquence—are both working against us today; one, Gaius Aquilius, causes me apprehension, the other fills me with dread. I am to a considerable degree bothered by the thought that the eloquence of Quintus Hortensius may hinder the effectiveness of my pleading this case; but I am in grave fear that the influence of Sextus Naevius may injure the cause of my client, Publius Quinctius. The possession of such advantages by our opponents to such a high degree would not seem so lamentable, if we possessed at least a modicum of either; but as it stands, I, who have insufficient experience and little natural ability, am matched against an advocate who is extremely skilled in speaking, while my client Quinctius, whose resources are scanty, who has no opportunities and only a meager contingent of friends, contends with a highly influential adversary. Moreover, we are working under yet another disadvantage: Marcus Junius, who has several times pleaded this case before you, who has great experience in other cases and has often and much been involved in this one, is prevented by his new appointment as legate from being here today. So, they had recourse to me, who, even if I were in consummate possession of other qualifications, have had scarcely enough time to be able to acquaint myself with the case, a case so important and complicated by so many disputed points. Thus, what has customarily been a help to me in other cases actually fails me in this one. For what I lack in natural ability, I have always made up for by my diligence; and how great this diligence is cannot really be appreciated, unless time and space have been granted.

The more numerous these disadvantages are, Aquilius, the more receptive you and your fellow assessors should be to listening to our words, so that the truth, debilitated by so many unfavorable conditions, might finally be revived by the impartiality of such eminent men. But if you as judge seem unable to provide any protection to isolation and need in the face of power and influence, if, before this council, the case depends on resources rather than on truth, then certainly nothing sacred, nothing pure any longer exists in the state, nothing by which the authority and virtue of the judge can console the humbleness of an ordinary citizen. Undoubtedly, either truth will prevail before you and your fellow assessors, or repelled from this place by power and influence, it will be unable to find a place on which to stand.

I do not speak in this way, Gaius Aquilius, because I doubt your trustworthiness and constancy, or because Publius Quinctius should not have the highest confidence in these most distinguished men of state whom you have called to assist you. What is it, then? First of all, the magnitude of the danger causes great fear in my client, seeing that all of his fortunes hang on this single judgment; and when he contemplates that fact, the thought of your power enters his mind no less often than that of your impartiality; for, as a rule, all those whose lives have been placed in the hands of another think more often about what the man under whose power and authority they find themselves is capable of doing, rather than what he ought to do. Second, Publius Quinctius has as his opponent Sextus Naevius in name, but in reality his opponents are men who are highly skilled in speaking, very bold, and most prosperous in our state, who defend Naevius with united efforts and vast resources —if "defending" actually means bowing to the desire of another party in order to be able the more easily to oppress anyone he wishes with an unfair trial. For what is more unfair or more disgraceful than the fact that I, who am defending the civil rights, the reputation, and the fortunes of the other party, should have to present my case first, especially when Quintus Hortensius, who in this trial assumes the role of an accuser, and whom nature has endowed with great talent and consummate fluency of speech, is going to speak against me? And so, it happens that I, who am obligated to ward off the weapons of the enemy and heal the wounds inflicted by them, am compelled to do so even before my adversary has launched any, while time is granted to them for staging an attack, when the power of avoiding their onslaught will have been snatched away from us, and when, if they hurl a false charge like some poisoned dart—as they are prepared to do—, there will be no opportunity for us to apply a suitable antidote. . . .

Since Publius Quinctius, weakened and afflicted by so many and such great difficulties, has taken refuge in your trustworthiness, Aquilius, in your honesty, in your compassion; and since up to this point in time the power of his adversaries has made it impossible for him to find equal justice or the same ability to present his case or an impartial magistrate; and since, by supreme injustice, all things have become dangerous and hostile to him, he begs and implores you, Aquilius, and you, members of this council, to allow impartiality, jostled and tossed about by many acts of injustice, to stand firm and regain its strength at last in this place. (*Pro P. Quinctio* 1–8, 10)

Narration or Statement of Facts
(*Latin* Narratio)

The second major part of a speech is the narration, or statement of facts (Latin, narratio). "Facts," of course, can be a slippery term, and the notion of imparting "spin" to a story is as old as speech itself. Each speaker attempts to state his version of the facts of the case in a way that will be most beneficial to his argument. Rhetorical handbooks tell us that the ideal narration should possess three qualities: brevity, clarity, and persuasiveness or plausibility. One of the finest examples of an effective narration in Cicero's corpus of speeches comes from his defense of Titus Annius Milo, who was accused of murdering his rival Publius Clodius (the same Clodius who had earlier instigated Cicero's exile), as their two parties met on the Appian Way in January of 52 BC. While this meeting probably occurred by chance, Cicero is intent on showing that his client, the unsuspecting Milo, was ambushed intentionally by Clodius, who then happened to be killed in the fray by Milo's loyal servants.

And in order that you might get a clearer view of this question, please listen carefully while I present a brief narrative of what transpired.

Publius Clodius had determined to harass the state by every sort of criminal means during his praetorship; he saw that the elections of the previous year had been postponed to such an extent that he would be able to hold his praetorship for only a few months; and unlike others, he did not really have regard for the high honor of such a political office, but rather was only interested in Lucius Paulus, a citizen of singular merit, not serving as his colleague, and in having a full year in which to tear the state to pieces. So he suddenly transferred his candidacy from his proper year to the following year, not, as often happens, because of some religious scruple, but, as he himself was declaring, in order to have a full and unbroken year to exercise his praetorship—that is to say, to overthrow the state.

It occurred to him that his praetorship would be crippled and debilitated were Milo to be elected consul; and he saw that Milo, by an overwhelming consensus of the Roman people, was, in fact, likely to become consul. He rushed to the support of Milo's fellow-candidates, but on the condition that he himself alone should direct the entire campaign, even if he should act against their will, and that he would, to use his own words, carry the whole election on his own shoulders. He assembled the tribes, he interposed himself, he enrolled a new Colline tribe through a levy of the most profligate citizens. But the more he stirred up trouble, day by day the stronger Milo grew. When Clodius, supremely on the ready for every sort of crime, saw that bravest of men, his bitterest foe, was a sure bet to become consul, when he realized that this fact had been declared not only in gossip but also by the votes of the Roman people, then he began to work openly and declare plainly that Milo had to be killed. He had brought down from the Apennines slaves, brutish and barbaric, who had laid waste to the public forests and harassed Etruria—you often saw them. The matter was not at all kept secret; for he was declaring openly that, while the consulship could not be taken from Milo, at least his life could. He indicated this often in the Senate; he stated it in public meetings. What is more, when that very courageous man Marcus Favonius asked him what he hoped for in his frenzy, as long as Milo lived, he responded that Milo would be dead in three, or at most four days—a remark that Favonius immediately reported to our friend here, Marcus Cato.

Meanwhile, since Clodius learned—and it was not difficult to learn from the Lanuvians—that Milo, as honorary dictator of Lanuvium, had to make a journey there, obligatory by ritual and law, on 18 January in order to declare the election of a flamen, he himself suddenly set out from

Rome on the day before, in order that—as the sequel revealed—he might lay an ambush for Milo in front of his estate; what is more, he set out under the circumstance of having to leave an uproarious public meeting that was being held on that day and that sorely missed his frenzied spirit, a meeting that he would have never left had he not wished to arrange with precision the time and place of his crime.

Milo, on the other hand, having spent the entire day in the Senate until its dismissal, went home, changed his shoes and clothes, waited for a time while his wife was getting ready, as often happens, then set out at a point in time when Clodius could have already returned to Rome, had he actually intended to do so on that day. He was met by Clodius, unencumbered, on horseback, no carriage, no baggage, no customary Greek companions in his retinue, without his wife (which almost never happened); our so-called conspirator here, on the other hand, who had allegedly planned that journey in order to commit murder, was riding in a carriage, dressed in a traveling cloak, accompanied by a huge, unwieldy, and largely female retinue composed primarily of maidservants and pages. He runs into Clodius in front of his estate at around five o'clock in the afternoon, or thereabout. Immediately several armed men, stationed on higher ground, make an attack on my client; others blocking the carriage, kill the coachman; but when Milo threw off his cloak, leapt from the carriage, and was defending himself with great courage, those who accompanied Clodius, with swords drawn, partly ran to the carriage in order to attack Milo from the rear, or partly, because they thought Milo had already been killed, began to cut down his slaves who were following. Among those slaves showing presence of mind and loyalty toward their master, some were killed, while others, when they saw the fight going on around the carriage and were prevented from helping their master, and when they heard from Clodius himself that Milo was killed and believed it to be true, Milo's slaves—for I will speak openly not in order to shift the charge, but to describe how it actually happened—Milo's slaves, I say, without the order or the knowledge or the presence of their master, did what everyone would have wished his own slaves to do in such a situation. (*Pro Milone* 23–29)

Confirmation or Proof
(*Latin* Confirmatio)

Proof of one's case, in which the orator relies chiefly on methods of rational argumentation for persuasion (see earlier, 19–24), generally follows the narration. On some occasions, the speaker may choose to introduce the confirmation with a partition (Latin partitio*), in which he briefly outlines what his agreements are with his opponents and what is left in dispute, or more often, mentions in a methodical way what he intends to discuss in the proof. Cicero, in his* De Inventione, *has this to say about the* confirmatio:

The confirmation or proof is that part of the speech through which our case gains credit, authority, and support through the marshaling of arguments. . . . All propositions are confirmed in argument by attributes of persons or attributes of actions. We consider the following to be attributes of persons: name, nature, manner of life, fortune, habit, feeling, interests, purposes, achievements, accidents, speeches made. . . . The attributes of actions are partly coherent with the action itself, partly considered in connection with the performance of the action, partly adjunct with the action, and partly consequent upon the performance of the action. . . . But every argument drawn from these common topics that we have mentioned will have to be either probable or irrefutable. For, to define it briefly, an argument seems to be something devised in order to demonstrate a point with probability or to prove it irrefutably. Those things are proved irrefutably that cannot happen or be proved otherwise than stated. . . . The probable is something that generally is accustomed to happen, or that is generally among people's ordinary beliefs, or contains in itself some resemblance to these qualities, whether that resemblance be true or false. (*De Inventione* 1.34, 37, 44, 46)

Cicero then goes on to elaborate on each of these categories and subdivisions. The following passage is taken from the confirmatio *of Cicero's speech on behalf of Milo (see earlier, 50–54); recall that in defending his client Milo, who is charged with murdering Clodius, Cicero is endeavoring to prove that Clodius actually set the ambush for Milo, who was merely defending himself against attack. This passage illustrates several arguments that rely on the principles of proof and argumentation mentioned by Cicero earlier, particularly on the notion of probability. In that connection, Cicero earlier in the speech had invoked the famous legal maxim of Cassius Longinus,* Cui bono *("To whose advantage?" or "Who stood to gain?"), a question invoked still today in court when attempting to establish the probability of motive. He resumes the theme here and continues with his arguments based on probability and advantage:*

Up to this point, gentlemen of the jury, I see that all the evidence points in one direction — that for Milo, it was actually advantageous for Clodius to continue to live, while for Clodius, the death of Milo was the realization of everything that he had so earnestly desired; that Clodius's hatred toward Milo was extremely bitter, while Milo harbored no hatred at all; that Clodius had made it a habit of relying on violence, while Milo was only in the habit of repelling it; that Clodius threatened and openly predicted Milo's death, while no such thing was heard from Milo; Clodius knew the day of Milo's departure, but Clodius's return was unknown to my client; Milo's journey was a matter of necessity,

Clodius's was relevant to nothing; Milo had announced openly that he would leave Rome on that day, while Clodius had concealed that he would return on that day; no detail of Milo's plan was changed, while Clodius had fabricated a reason for altering his; Milo, if he were the one laying the ambush, would have had to wait for nightfall near the city, while Clodius, even if he had no fear of Milo, would still have had reason to fear approaching the city by night.

Let us now examine the key factor in this whole affair, namely which party had a more advantageous position for an ambush in the place where they actually met. On this point, jurors, must we still continue to doubt and waste more time in thought? Was it in front of Clodius's estate—a place where, thanks to those insanely huge foundations, a thousand able-bodied men were easily accommodated—that Milo judged he would have an advantage over his adversary who was stationed in a high commanding position, and so he accordingly chose that of all places for the fight? Was it not rather that my client was waited for at that very spot by one who, owing to his confidence in that location, had planned to make the attack there? Facts speak for themselves, gentlemen of the jury, facts always powerfully prevail. If you were not hearing a narrative of these events, but rather were viewing them in a painting, it would still be patently clear which man was the one laying an ambush and which was the one harboring no evil designs — this one riding in a carriage, encumbered by a heavy cloak, and sitting next to his wife. Which of these could be more of a hindrance — garment, vehicle, traveling companion? What could render someone less prepared for battle than to be entangled by a cloak, encumbered by a carriage, almost chained to a wife? Look now at Clodius, first proceeding from his villa, suddenly — why? In the evening — why was that a necessity? In a leisurely fashion — how does that fit, especially at that time of day? "He was paying a visit to Pompeius's villa." Was it to see Pompeius? But he knew that Pompeius was at his place at Alsium. Was it to take a look at the villa? But he had been in that villa a thousand times. What was it, then? Nothing but delay and dilly-dallying: he didn't want to leave the spot until Milo should arrive.

Next, please, compare the mode of travel of this unencumbered hoodlum with Milo's baggage. Clodius had always before traveled with his wife;

now he is without her; never before, except in a carriage; now he is on horseback. Greek minions with him wherever he went, even when he was hurrying out to his Etrurian operations; now no trace of such trifles in his retinue. Milo, who never bothered with such people, had with him on this occasion some of his wife's choristers and flocks of handmaids; Clodius, who always brought with him harlots, male prostitutes, and whores, on this occasion traveled with none other than those you would describe as hand-picked men.

Why, then, was he defeated? Because the traveler is not always killed by the highwayman; sometimes even the highwayman is killed by the traveler; and because, although a prepared Clodius had fallen upon the unprepared, Clodius himself nonetheless was a woman who had fallen upon men. (*Pro Milone* 52–55)

Refutation (*Latin* Refutatio)

Going hand in hand with proof of your case or argument is the refutation of your opponent's argument:

Then support for the case must be built by demolishing your opponent's arguments and by proving your own at the same time. For in every case, the portion of the speech that serves to establish your argumentation is, so to speak, based on just one principle. This portion does require both proof and refutation, but since you cannot refute the opponent's points without proving your own, nor prove your own without refuting your opponent's, it follows that these things are closely connected in terms of their nature, their usefulness, and their treatment. (*De oratore* 2.331)

In On Invention, *Cicero outlines four ways by which to refute your opponent's argument:*

Every argument is refuted in one of these ways: if one or more of its assumptions is not granted; or if the assumptions are granted, it is denied that a conclusion can be drawn from them; or the actual form of argument is shown to be fallacious; or a strong argument is countered by one equally strong or stronger. (*De inventione* 1.79)

In 62 BC, Cicero defended a friend, former teacher, and native Greek, Archias, on a charge of claiming Roman citizenship falsely, a charge that, if proven, would have resulted in Archias's expulsion from Rome. In the following excerpt, Cicero refutes claims that have been made, or will likely be made by the prosecution.

If the validity of Archias's citizenship and his compliance with the relevant law are the points at issue, I need say nothing more—the defense rests. For can you refute either of these points, Grattius? Will you deny that Archias was enrolled as a citizen at that time in Heraclea? Marcus Lucullus, a man of highest authority, scruple, and honor, is present; he testifies not that he thinks, but knows, not that he heard but saw, not that he was merely present but that he acted as agent. A delegation from Heraclea is present, highly distinguished men, who have come to Rome for this trial, with writs and public testimony, to declare that Archias was enrolled. At this point, my opponent asks for the public archives of Heraclea to be produced, archives we all know were destroyed in the burning of the record-office during the War with the Allies. It is absurd to say nothing about the evidence that we have, but seek evidence that we cannot possibly obtain; to remain silent about the record of living men, but demand a written record should be produced; and, although you have at your disposal the scrupulousness of a very noble man and the sworn oath and testimony of an incorruptible municipality, to reject such things—which in no way can be corrupted—but ask for public records, which you yourself admit are regularly subject to tampering.

Or do you deny that my client had established permanent residence in Rome—that is, the man who had, for so many years before he had been granted citizenship, made Rome the depository of all his property and fortunes? Or did he fail to register? On the contrary, he did register, and what is more, out of those declarations made then, his are the only ones from that registration and that board of magistrates that still have the authority of actual public records. For, although the citizen rolls of Appius were allegedly kept somewhat carelessly, and although all trustworthiness of such records had been impaired by the unreliability of Gabinius, . . . yet Metellus, the most upright and scrupulous man of all, was so diligent in his record-keeping that he actually came to Lucius Lentulus the praetor, and a jury, and declared that he was deeply troubled by the erasure of a single entry. Here are the records, and you will see that there is no erasure by the name of Archias. . . .

You say that you search in vain for Archias's name on our census-rolls. To be sure! I suppose it's a great secret that during the last census he was with the army as a staff member to the illustrious general Lucius Lucullus; and at the time of the previous census, he was with Lucullus again, who was then serving as quaestor in Asia; and previous to that, when Julius and Crassus were in office, no census of any section of the populace was held. But, since the census-roll does not confirm citizenship, and in fact merely indicates that one whose name is on the roll was then conducting himself in the manner of a citizen, please note that at that time my client, whom you allege, even in his own judgment, to have had no rights as a Roman citizen, had often made his will in accordance with Roman law, had entered upon inheritances left to him by Roman citizens, and had been recommended to the treasury for a reward by Lucius Lucullus, the proconsul. Search for arguments if you can find any; for Archias will never be convicted of falsehood—neither by his own judgment, nor that of his friends. (*Pro Archia* 8–11)

Conclusion or Epilogue
(*Latin* Conclusio or Peroratio)

The final part of a standard speech or argument is the conclusion or epilogue, during which you can sum up or recapitulate previous arguments and/ or stir the listeners' emotions, either by exciting indignation against your opponent, or arousing pity or sympathy for you or your client. As a result, the epilogue is a favorite portion of a speech for employing pathos *as a primary mode of persuasion (see earlier, 32–36). We have already included a* pathos-*laden passage from the epilogue of Cicero's speech on behalf of Plancius (see earlier, 36–40).*

The following excerpt comes from the peroration of Cicero's speech on behalf of his young protégé, Marcus Caelius, delivered in 56 BC. Although Caelius was charged on five counts, including violence and attempted poisoning, Cicero based his defense to a large extent on arguing that the charges had actually been trumped up by a woman behind the scenes, Clodia, sister of Cicero's arch-enemy Clodius (see earlier, 50), who was, according to Cicero's account, Caelius's older, conniving, and vindictive ex-lover. Cicero argues that Caelius has sown his wild oats and is now ready to follow in his mentor's footsteps, assuming a role of leadership in the state. Noteworthy here, in addition, are Cicero's efforts at both stirring up indignation against Caelius's (and Cicero's) enemies, and evoking pity and sympathy by introducing into the court Caelius's elderly father.

I have stated my case, jurors, and my speech has now come to its conclusion. You surely understand how weighty a verdict you are deliberating and how grave a matter has been entrusted to you. You are deliberating on a charge of violence. And the law concerning violence pertains directly to the power, to the majesty, to the condition of our country, to the safety of all. It is the law that Quintus Catulus proposed when there was an armed rebellion of citizens, at nearly the state's most desperate time; it is the law that, after the fire that blazed forth during my consulship, extinguished the smoldering embers of the conspiracy; it is now the same law by which the youthful life of Caelius is demanded for punishment, not by the state but by the depraved sport and caprice of a woman. . . .

Preserve for our country, therefore, jurors, a citizen of virtuous principles, a loyal citizen, a patriotic citizen. I promise you this and this I pledge to the state that, if I myself have served it well, he will never be separated from my way of thinking. And I can promise this, both relying on our close friendship and because he has now bound himself on the strictest of terms: one who has called into court an ex-consul, charging that he has violated the state, cannot himself be a seditious citizen in that state; again, one who does not allow a man's acquittal on a charge of bribery to stand, cannot himself ever offer a bribe with impunity. Our state has two judicial accusations from Marcus Caelius, accusations that can be considered hostages against dangerous behavior on his part, or rather pledges of his good will. And so, jurors, I beg and plead with you that, in this state, where only a few days ago Sextus Cloelius was acquitted—a man whom, for the past two years, you have witnessed as either the servant or the leader of sedition, a man without property or credit, without hope or home or resources, a man whose tongue, hands, and entire life are foully polluted, who with his own hands burned down a sacred shrine—the depository of the census, the records of the Roman people—who inflicted damage on the monument of Catulus, tore down my house, and set fire to my brother's, who on the Palatine in view of the whole city incited slaves to murder and arson—in this same state, do not allow that man to have been acquitted through the influence of a woman, and Caelius to have been sacrificed to the passion of a woman, so that one and the same woman, in league with her brother and "husband," does not appear to have both rescued the foulest of criminals and to have crushed the most honorable of youths.

And when you consider the youth of Caelius, set before your eyes also the old age of this poor man, who relies on his only son, who is supported by his hope for him, who fears for his downfall. Mindful of the memory of your own parents and the fondness you have for your own children, sustain this man, a suppliant of your mercy, prostrate not so much before your feet as he is before your hearts and sensibilities, so that, in the suffering of another, you might do service to your own sense of dutifulness and forgiveness. Do not willingly snuff out this old man's life, already naturally approaching its end, more quickly by your blow than by fate's; nor uproot, as if by some whirlwind or sudden tempest, this young man's life, now in its prime, blossoming with virtue. Save the son for the parent and the parent for the son, lest you seem either to have despised an old man, now almost desperate, or lest you appear not only not to have nourished, but actually to have crushed and destroyed a youth, full of highest hopes. If you preserve Caelius for me, for his own people, and for our state, you will have one who is pledged, devoted, and bound fast to you and to your children; it is you above all, jurors, who will reap the rich and abiding fruits of all of his energy and endeavors. (*Pro Caelio* 70, 77–80)

Style

The third part of rhetoric, or the third activity of the orator, is style (Latin elocutio*). After you have planned what to say (invention) and have decided on the order in which to say it (arrangement), you must decide* how *to say it, by casting your subject matter into language—actual words and sentences. The same subject matter can obviously be*

expressed in different words and in different man-
ners, so the object of this third activity is to choose
effective words and to connect those words into
sentences, employing periodic structure, prose
rhythm (an important consideration in ancient
oratory), and figures of speech. In his De oratore,
Cicero is emphatic about the inseparable bond
between subject matter and expression, that is,
between content and words. Verbiage that flows
without having its origin in knowledge of the
subject matter is empty and ridiculous, while
even brilliant content can be obscured by a poor
choice of words and their ineffectual connection:

For since all discourse is made up of content
and words, the words cannot have any basis if
you withdraw the content, and the content will
remain in the dark if you remove the words. . . .
Eloquence forms a unity, into whatever realms
or areas of discourse it travels: whether it is
speaking about the nature of the heavens or
of the earth, or about divine or human nature,
whether in trials, in the Senate, or from the rostra, whether its purpose is to urge people on or
to teach them or to deter them, or to stir them
or to curb them, or to kindle their emotions or

to calm them, whether its audience be few or many, or strangers or one's friends or oneself: speech is like a river, branching out into little streams, yet issuing from the same source; and in whatever direction it goes, it is attended by the same equipment and adornment. But we are now laboring under the opinions not only of the crowd, but also of half-educated people. They find it easier to deal with things they cannot grasp in their entirety, if they split them apart and almost tear them to pieces, and they separate words from thoughts just like a body from its soul—which in both cases can only wreak destruction. In my discussion, therefore, I will undertake no more than is assigned to me. I would only indicate briefly that discovering words for a distinguished style is impossible without having produced and shaped the thoughts, and that no thought can shine clearly without the enlightening power if words. (*De oratore* 3.19, 22–24)

There is, of course, no single style that is alone excellent, no single way of choosing words and configuring them into sentences that is superior to all others. Cicero recognizes this point and is emphatic in stressing that each speaker's individual strengths and weaknesses must be ascertained, and appropriate stylistic proclivities encouraged and developed in each case—salutary advice for teachers still today:

Between all of us here, then, there are great differences, and each of us has clear and specific traits. And amid this variety, the better is generally distinguished from the worse more by ability than by the type to which each belongs, and everything that is perfect in its own type is praised. So don't you think that if we chose to include all orators who are or have ever been active anywhere, we would have to say something like, "as many orators, so many styles of speaking"?

Perhaps my argument will give rise to a further notion: if there is indeed an almost countless number of, let us say, forms and kinds of speaking, different in appearance but praiseworthy in their own types, then these mutually different things cannot be molded by the same rules and by one method of instruction. But this is not true. It is the responsibility of those who provide instruction and education to observe very carefully where each pupil's natural abilities seem to lead him. In fact, when we look at the schools run by expert teachers who were superior in their own different types, we see that each one produced pupils who were different from one another and still praiseworthy, since every teacher adapted his instruction to the natural abilities of each individual pupil. The most striking example of this (to leave aside other arts) is probably that the incomparable teacher Isocrates said that he always used the spurs on Ephorus, but the reins on Theopompus. He checked the latter, who was unrestrained in his bold use of words, while he urged on the former, who was hesitant and modest, so to speak. Yet he did not make them alike; he added to the one and pared away from the other only as much as was necessary to reinforce in each what his natural abilities allowed. (*De oratore* 3.34–36)

Discussions concerning style in Cicero's time were usually organized either around the four qualities or "virtues" of style as defined by Aristotle's student Theophrastus, or according to three or more "types" or "characters." The virtues of style are the correct use of Greek (or Latin in Cicero's case; English, in ours), clarity, distinction (ornamentation), which includes tropes such as metaphors, figures of speech, and figures of thought, and appropriateness. The best-known categorization of "types" or "characters" of style is the threefold division into "plain," "middle," and "grand."

Virtues of Style

CORRECTNESS AND CLARITY

In De oratore *(3.37–41, 48–49), Cicero's interlocutor, Crassus, speaks briefly about the first two qualities of style and makes it clear that all literate speakers are already in possession of these virtues, though study and further reading of the orators and poets will strengthen and enhance them.*

And tell me, is there a better way of expression . . . than to speak correct Latin, clearly, with distinction, and in a manner that is suitable and appropriate to the particular matter at issue? Now I don't think that I am expected to give an account of the two elements that I mentioned first, pure and lucid language. For we do not attempt to teach someone to speak who doesn't know how to talk, and we cannot hope, if someone cannot speak correct Latin, that he is going to speak with distinction—or, for that matter, if someone cannot say something that we might understand, that he will be able to say something that we might admire. . . . Still, every aspect of refined diction, though it can be polished by a knowledge of grammar, can nonetheless be developed by reading the orators and the poets. For almost all of the ancients, though they were not yet able to impart distinction to what they said, expressed themselves very well, and people who have become accustomed to their language cannot fail to speak anything but correct Latin, even if they should try. This is not to say that we should employ the words that are not employed in normal usage anymore, except sparingly, for the sake of imparting distinction to what we say, as I will point out later. But in the employment of words in common use you will be able to use the choicest among them if you have thoroughly and devotedly immersed yourself in the writings of the ancients.

But in order to speak correct Latin, we must not only be careful to utter words that no one might justifiably criticize, and to use them in the proper case, tense, class, and number, so that there is no confusion, want of agreement, or incorrect order; but we must also control our tongue, our breath, and the actual sound of our voice. I don't like letters to be overarticulated with too much affectation, and I don't like them to be obscured by being pronounced too carelessly; I don't like words to sound thin by being pronounced with too little breath, and I don't like them to be puffed up and uttered, as it were, with too full and heavy a breath. . . .

Let us, then, pass over the rules for speaking correct Latin, which are taught in our elementary lessons, fostered by a more precise, systematic knowledge of grammar, or by the practice of daily conversation at home, and strengthened by books and the reading of the ancient orators and poets. And really, let us not spend more time on the second point, on discussing in what ways we can see to it that what we say will be understood—obviously by speaking correct Latin, by employing words in common use that properly designate the things we want to be signified and indicated, by avoiding ambiguous words or language, excessively long periodic sentences, and spun-out metaphors, by not breaking up the train of thought, confusing the chronology, mixing up people, or muddling the order.

DISTINCTION (ORNAMENTATION)

The third quality of style, distinction or ornamentation, traditionally received the most attention by ancient rhetorical theorists. Included in this category are things such as tropes or "turnings," that is, substitutions of one term for another as in metaphor; changes in the sequence or sounds of words, that is, figures of speech such as alliteration or anaphora; figures of thought such as rhetorical question, designed to emphasize a thought or involve the audience more directly; and cadence and rhythm, the effective arrangement of our words to render not strict metrical patterns, but rhythms that make our prose pleasing to the ear. As mentioned earlier, Cicero felt strongly that style must be rooted firmly in content—in fact, that it actually resides in content, rather than being something that is applied artificially like cosmetics. And like all things that are truly distinctive, judicial use and tasteful variation are the secrets to a truly distinctive style.

Distinction, then, is imparted to a speech in the first place by its general character and its own particular complexion and vitality, as it were. That it should be weighty, charming, and learned, that it should be well-bred, admirable, and accomplished, and that it should contain as much feeling and emotion as necessary—this is not a matter of the individual limbs, but these qualities are discerned in the body as a whole. That it should, as the next point, be sprinkled, as it were, with flowers of language and thought, this is a quality that must not be spread evenly throughout the entire speech, but must be distributed here and there in the way that decorations and lights are arranged when a public place is adorned. We must, then, choose a general character for our speech that will do most to hold the attention of our audience, and that not only delights them, but does so without causing satiety. . . . It is difficult to say why the very things that most stir our senses with pleasure and rouse them most strongly when we first encounter them are also the quickest to give us feelings of aversion and satiety, and thus to alienate us. How much brighter than old paintings are most of the modern ones, with their beauty and variety of color! Yet, even if they captivate us at first glance, they do not delight us much longer, whereas, on the contrary, our attention is held precisely by the roughness and the fainter colors of ancient paintings. In singing, how much softer and more delicate are the coloratura and falsetto notes than unadorned ones firmly held! Yet, not only people of more austere tastes dislike them, but even the crowd shouts its disapproval if they are heard too often. You can also see this in the other senses. Perfumes with an intense and penetratingly sweet scent do not delight us for so long as the moderately sweet ones, and what seems to have the fragrance of wax receives more praise than what hints of saffron. Even with the sense of touch, there is a limit to softness and smoothness. Yes, even our taste, the sense that is most responsive to pleasure and that is roused by sweetness more than the other senses—how quickly does it spurn and reject what is intensely sweet! Surely nobody can take sweet food or drink for too long? But both food and drink that affect this sense with only light feelings of pleasure quite easily avoid causing feelings of satiety. Since in everything else, then, the greatest pleasure borders on aversion, we need not be too surprised by this phenomenon in the case of speech. Here, our experience with poets as well as orators allows us to conclude that poetry or prose that is elegant, decorated, distinguished, and pretty, but continuously so without new starts or variety, cannot give delight for a very long time, however vivid the colors in which it is painted. In fact, people take offense more quickly at the curls and cosmetics of an orator or poet, for the following reason: satiety of the senses stemming from excessive pleasure is a matter of nature, not of the mind, while in the case of the written and the spoken word, faults of overcoloring are not only recognized through the judgment of the ears, but even more through that of the intellect.

Accordingly, I don't mind hearing people say "great!" and "outstanding!" about us, however often, but I don't like to hear "charming!" or "how pretty!" too often. Certainly, the popular exclamation, "couldn't be better!" I would want to hear repeatedly. All the same, such admiration during a speech, this highest praise, should have some areas of shade and some recesses, so that what is highlighted can be seen to stand out more prominently. (*De oratore* 3.96–101)

APPROPRIATENESS

The fourth quality or virtue of style is appropriateness or propriety, that is, fitting to your speech

or argument the most appropriate style for that
particular occasion, opponent, or audience.

It is, of course, obvious that no single style is
fitting for every case or every audience or every
person involved or every occasion. Cases in
which someone's civic status is at issue require
one specific tone, while private and insignificant
cases require another. Deliberative speeches,
laudatory speeches, lawsuits, conversations, con-
solations, rebukes, discussions, and the writing of
history all demand different styles. It also makes
a difference who our audience is—whether it is
the Senate, the people, or a jury, whether it is
large, small, or an individual, and what sort of
people they are. The speakers themselves must
also be considered: their age, their prestige, and
how much authority they possess. As to the occasion, is it peace or war, is there some urgency
or is there room for a leisurely approach? So it
seems that there is really no rule that I could give
you at this point, except that when choosing a
type of speech—a fuller or a more slender one,
or indeed the middle type—we should see to it
that it is adapted to the problem at hand; and we
may in each case employ approximately the same

elements for imparting distinction, sometimes more energetically, at other times in a lower key. In every area, the capacity to do what is appropriate is a matter of art and natural ability, but to know what is appropriate at each time is a matter of good sense. (*De oratore* 3.210–12)

In his Orator *(70–74), Cicero elaborates on this point in a more philosophical and reflective manner:*

The foundation of eloquence, just as of everything else, is wisdom. In a speech, just as in life, nothing is more difficult than to discern what is appropriate. The Greeks call it *prepon*; let us call it "appropriateness." Many brilliant precepts have been handed down about this, and this subject is most worthy of our consideration. Ignorance of what is appropriate causes mistakes not only in life but very often also in poetry and public speaking. Moreover, the speaker must pay attention to appropriateness not only in his thoughts but also even in his words. For not every station in life, not every rank, not every position, not every age, nor every time or place or audience should be treated with the same style of words or thoughts: in every part of our speech, as in every part of life, we must consider what is appropriate; and this depends on the subject matter that is being discussed as well as on the characters of the speakers and the listeners. Thus, the philosophers are accustomed to treat this extensive topic under the subject of moral duties (though not when they are discussing absolute virtue, for that is one and unchanging); teachers of literature consider it in connection with poetry; eloquent speakers in dealing with every kind and every part of their case. How inappropriate it is to employ general topics and amplified language when, before a single judge, you are pleading a case about the drainage of rainwater, or to use a low-key, submissive tone when speaking about the majesty of the Roman people. These err in every respect, while others make a mistake in terms of character, either their own, or that of the jurors, or of their opponents— and not only in substance but often in the use of words. Although a word has no force apart from the thing, the same thing is still often either approved or rejected depending on its being expressed by one word or another. And in all cases, the question must be, "How far?" For, although each subject has its own limits of appropriateness, too much is generally more offensive than too little. And Apelles used to say that those painters who do not have a sense of what is enough also make the same mistake. . . . But if the poet avoids inappropriateness as the greatest fault and even makes a mistake when he places the speech of an upright man in the mouth of a villain or that of a wise man in the mouth of a fool; or if a painter, in a scene of the sacrifice of Iphigenia, when he has portrayed Calchas as sad, Ulysses as more sad, and Menelaus as grieving, recognizes that Agamemnon's head must be veiled since his supreme sorrow could not be captured by his brush; if finally even the actor searches for what is appropriate—what then do we think the orator should do? Since this is of such importance, let the orator consider what to do in his cases and in their various parts: it is certainly obvious that not only the different parts of a speech, but even entire cases must be handled now in one style, now in another.

Types or Characters of Style

An alternative way to discuss style was to classify it according to various types or "characters," most commonly three, the plain, middle, and grand.

Cicero employs this classification in the Orator, *but takes it a step further by adding a unique and original variation: he correlates the Aristotelian artistic sources of proof,* logos, ethos, *and* pathos *(see earlier, 15–17) with the Latin verbs* pro-bare *(to prove),* delectare *(to delight or to charm), and* flectere *(to sway), and identifies each with one of the stylistic types.*

The eloquent speaker whom we seek will be the one who will speak in the forum and the courts in such a way as to prove and to delight and to sway. To prove is a necessity, to delight adds charm, to sway brings victory—for of all things this one is the most potent weapon for winning cases. For these three functions of the speaker there are three styles, the plain style for proving, the middle style for delighting, and the vigorous style for swaying; and in this last re-sides the full force of a speaker. The one who manages and, as it were, combines these three different styles will need to be in possession of keen judgment and very high ability; for he will judge what is required in any situation, and will be able to speak in whatever way the case de-mands. (*Orator* 69–70)

While it is clear that Cicero favors the grand style as the one that possesses the most power and persuasive weight, he insists that the best speakers should be masters of all three styles, knowing how and when to employ each, and how to modulate them accordingly. A steady diet of the grand style, for example, will only lead to disaster.

The speaker of the grand style is abundant, copious, stately, and distinctive, and he certainly wields the greatest power. For this is the speaker whose distinctiveness and fluency of speech have caused admiring nations to allow eloquence to hold sway in the state; and this is the sort of eloquence that rushes on its course with a mighty roar, that all extol, that all admire, that all despair of attaining. This eloquence plies the hearts of people and moves them in every possible way. This eloquence now shatters the senses, now insinuates itself into them; it sows new ideas and uproots firmly planted ones. But there is a great difference between this style and the others. One who has worked diligently on the plain and incisive style so as to speak with skill and accuracy, and has not contemplated anything higher, is, in respect to the perfection of this single style, a great orator—though not the greatest; he will not find himself on slippery ground, and once he has taken a stand, he will never fall. The speaker of the middle style, whom I call moderate and tempered, will not fear the doubtful and uncertain hazards of speaking, provided he has deployed his forces satisfactorily; even if, as often happens, he is not completely successful, he still will not be in great danger, for he cannot fall very far. But this speaker of ours whom we deem the chief—stately, fierce, and fiery—if he has inborn talent for this alone, or has trained himself in this one style, or has studied only this and does not temper his copiousness with the other two styles, is much to be despised. For the speaker in the plain style, because he speaks accurately and adroitly, is considered wise; the one employing the middle style is charming; but the very copious speaker, if there is nothing else to him, tends to appear insufficiently sane. For someone who can say nothing calmly, nothing mildly, nothing in an organized way, precisely, distinctly, or wittily—especially when some cases demand such treatment entirely, and others largely so—if he begins to inflame the situation without first preparing the ears of his audience, he appears to be nothing more than a raving maniac among the sane, a drunken reveler in the midst of the sober. (*Orator* 97–99)

The Rhetorica ad Herennium *or* Rhetoric to Herennius *was preserved among the works of Cicero and was, for a millennium, believed to be from his hand. Scholars from the Renaissance on, however, realized that the work was not authored by Cicero, though its content and date are, in fact, very close to those of Cicero's youthful work,* De inventione. *In any case, the anonymous author of the* ad Herennium *classifies style according to the categories of grand, middle, and plain, and gives the following examples of each:*

A speech will be composed in the grand style if for each and every idea the most distinctive words that can be found, whether literal or figurative, are employed; and if impressive thoughts, such that are used in amplification and appeals to pity, are chosen; and if we apply figures of thought and speech, which have weightiness. Here is an example of this type of style:

Who is there among you, jurors, who can think up a suitable punishment for him who has thought how to betray his country to our enemies? What evil-doing can be compared to this crime, what punishment can be found worthy of this evil-doing? On those who had done violence to a free-born youth, who had raped the mother of a family, who had wounded, or even killed someone, our ancestors expended their greatest punishments; for this most ferocious and nefarious crime they left us no specific penalty. In other evil-doing, injury arising from another's crime extends to an individual, or to only a few; but those complicit in this crime are, in one plot, devising the most atrocious disasters for all citizens. O such savage hearts! O such cruel designs! O such humans devoid of all humanity! What have they dared to do, or what can they be planning? They are planning how our enemies, after tearing up the graves of our ancestors and throwing down our walls, will rush in against our city with shouts of triumph; how, after the temples of the gods have been despoiled, the patriots butchered, others hauled off into slavery, mothers of families and freeborn youth subjected to enemy lust, the city, put to the torch in a most violent conflagration, will fall! They do not think they have accomplished the result they desire, unless they have looked upon the pitiable ashes of our most holy homeland. I cannot capture in words, jurors, the vileness of the thing; but I am rather unconcerned about it, because you have no need of me. Indeed your own spirit, full of patriotism for the Republic, indisputably instructs you to cast out this man, who wanted to betray the fortunes of all, headlong from the state, which he wanted to bury under the nefarious domination of the filthiest of enemies.

A speech will belong to the middle type if . . . we have relaxed our style to some degree, but still have not descended to the most ordinary prose, as follows:

You see, jurors, against whom we are waging war—against allies who have been accustomed to fight on our behalf and with us to preserve our empire by their virtue and industry. These men necessarily knew their own capabilities, supplies, and resources, but also, because of their nearness to us and their alliance with us in all affairs, they were no less able to know and assess the power of the Roman people in every respect. When they had made the decision to wage war against us, on what, I ask you, did they rely in presuming to undertake the war, since they realized that the vast majority of our allies were remaining faithful to their obligation, and since they saw that they had no multitude of soldiers, no suitable commanders, and no public money—in short, none of the things essential for carrying on a war? Even if they were waging a war with their neighbors over their boundaries, or even if they believed that the entire contest hinged on one battle, they would still come to the fight better prepared and better equipped in every way. It is even less conceivable that with such a tiny force at hand they would attempt to transfer to themselves sovereignty over the whole world, a sovereignty to which all nations, kings, and races have submitted, in part through force, in part through their own will, when conquered either by the arms or the generosity of the Roman people. "What about the Fregellans?" someone will ask. "Did they not make such an attempt on their own initiative?" Indeed, they did, but these allies would make such an attempt less readily because they saw how things turned out for the Fregellans. For those without experience in things, who are unable to find precedents for every circumstance in events that have transpired previously, are through imprudence very easily led into error; but those who know what has happened to others can, from events that have affected these others, easily provide for their own affairs. Have they, therefore, taken up arms, induced by no motive or relying on no hope? Who could believe this—that anyone had been seized by so much insanity as to dare, relying on no forces, to assail the sovereignty of the Roman people? Some motive, therefore, must have necessarily existed, and what else can it be but what I claim?

The following will serve as an example of the plain style, which is lowered to the level of everyday speech:

Our friend here happened to enter the baths, and after he washed, started to be rubbed down. Next, when he decided to get into the tub, this guy turns up out of nowhere. "Hey there, young fellow, your slaves just now gave me a pummeling, and you better make good on it." The young man blushed, for at his age he was not used to being called out by name by a total stranger. This guy began to repeat the same thing, but more loudly, and to add other things. The youth was barely able to reply, "Ok, let me look into it." But then this creep cries out in that tone of his that would easily cause anyone to blush—so pert and harsh—such as you would hear, if you ask me, not even in the neighborhood of the Sundial, but backstage and in other such places. The youth was upset, and no wonder, seeing that up till now his young ears were used to scoldings by his tutor, not wranglings of this sort. For where would our young man have seen such a stooge, who had forgotten how to blush and who thought that he had nothing left to lose from his good name, so that he could do anything at all without detriment to his reputation?

The types of style, therefore, can be understood from the examples themselves. For one arrangement of words is of the plain style, another belongs to the grand, and another to the middle. (*Rhetorica ad Herennium* 4.11–15)

In his Orator, *Cicero offers three of his own speeches as examples of the plain, middle, and grand style:*

My defense on behalf of Caecina (*Pro Caecina*) concerned itself entirely with the words of the praetor's provisional order: we explained

complicated matters through the process of definition, praised the civil law, and drew distinc-
tions between ambiguous terms. In the *Manilian
Law* (*Pro Lege Manilia*), glorification of Pompey was the goal: we set forth that glorification
richly with a speech in the middle style. My
defense of Rabirius (*Pro Rabirio*) was involved
with all aspects of the principle of upholding the
dignity of the state: in this speech, therefore, we
blazed forth in every manner of rhetorical amplification. (*Orator* 102)

*In the following extract from his speech on be-
half of Caecina, Cicero employs the plain style
as he endeavors to demonstrate the inadequacy
of words in describing complicated or subtle legal
concepts; the spirit of the law must take precedence over its letter:*

What statute, what senatorial decree, what
edict of magistrates, what treaty or agreement
or—to return to private concerns—what will,
what judgments or covenants or pacts or for-
mal agreements cannot be invalidated and torn
apart, if we are willing to reduce their meaning
to mere words, while abandoning the design, the

intention, and the authority of those who wrote them? Believe me, our familiar everyday speech will lack all coherence if we set traps with words for one another. . . . Cannot each and every one of you come up with some example, in one connection or another, that bears witness to the contention that Right does not depend on words, but that words are in the service of people's designs and intentions? Shortly before I became active in the forum, Lucius Crassus, by far the most eloquent of men, defended this opinion amply, distinctively, and indisputably; and although that very wise man Quintus Mucius Scaevola was speaking on the other side of the case, Crassus proved to everyone that Manius Curius, who had been named heir "in the event of the death of a posthumous son," was entitled to be named heir although the son was not dead—since, in fact, a son had never been born! Well, did the wording of the will provide sufficiently for such a situation? Not in the least. Then what was the deciding factor? Intention—for if our intentions were able to be understood while we remained silent, we would not use words at all; but because this is not possible, words have been invented, not to conceal but to reveal intention.

By statute, two years' possession determines property in land; but we employ the same principle in dealing with buildings, which are not specifically named in the statute. By statute, if a road is impassible, a person can drive his beast of burden by any road he chooses; relying merely on the wording, this could be taken to mean that if a road in Bruttium is impassible, a person may, if he chooses, drive his beast of burden through Marcus Scaurus's estate at Tusculum! A form of action can be brought against a vendor, if present in court, beginning with these words: "Since I see you in court. . . ." The legendary Appius Claudius, who was blind, could not use this form of action, if in court people adhered literally to the words without considering the actual meaning that the words are meant to express. If, in a will, "Cornelius the Minor" had been named the heir, and Cornelius were now twenty years old, he would lose his inheritance according to your interpretation. (*Pro Caecina* 51–54)

In 66 BC, the year of Cicero's praetorship, Gaius Manilius, one of the tribunes, proposed a law granting the general Pompey supreme command over the province of Asia (that is, Asia Minor)

and in the war against Mithridates, King of Pon-
tus. Cicero spoke in favor of the law, and he later
cites this speech as a prime example of the mid-
dle style. His task, as he says, was to praise the
character and ability of the general, a sample of
which we see in the following passage:

Come, now, consider the moderation that char-
acterizes Pompey in other situations. On what do
you think he has founded that great quickness
of his and that incredible speed of movement?
For it was not the extraordinary power of his
oarsmen, nor some unheard of skill in navigat-
ing, nor some strange winds that brought him
so quickly to the remotest of lands; rather, it
was the fact that the things accustomed to delay
others did not slow him down: Greed did not
lure him from his appointed course to some sort
of plunder, nor lust to some desire, nor pleasant prospect to some delight, nor the fame of
some city to its investigation, nor labor itself to
the opportunity for rest; finally, as to the statues
and paintings and other adornments of Greek
towns that the majority of generals think should
be carried off—Pompey judged that he should
not even view them. Now, for these reasons, all

people in those places look upon Gnaeus Pompeius as someone not sent from this city, but as one come down from heaven; now at last they are beginning to believe that there were once Romans who were characterized by this sort of self-control—something that already seemed incredible to foreign nations, and merely attributable to a mistaken memory; now the splendor of your empire has begun to shed its light on those peoples: now they understand that it was not without cause that their ancestors in those days, when we had magistrates of similar moderation, preferred to serve Rome rather than to rule others. Now, indeed, access to him by ordinary people is said to be so easy, the lodging of complaints over wrongs committed by others so open, that he who excels princes in terms of dignity seems to be equal to the lowliest in terms of accessibility. Now, how powerful he is in counsel, how powerful he is in the weight and eloquence of his oratory—which in itself is indicative of the dignity that is appropriate to a general—you have often, fellow citizens, had the opportunity to recognize in this very place. And his trustworthiness—how greatly do you think this is esteemed by our allies, when every enemy of every race has judged it absolutely unimpeachable? Now, he is marked by such humanity that it would be difficult to say whether warring enemies feared his valor more than the vanquished esteemed his clemency. Indeed, will anyone doubt that the conduct of such a great war should be entrusted to this man, who seems by some sort of divine design to have been born to bring all the wars within our memory to a conclusion? (*Pro Lege Manilia* 40–42)

In 63 BC, the year of Cicero's consulship, an aged senator, Gaius Rabirius, was indicted on a charge of high treason for actions that allegedly occurred some 36 years earlier. The charge was actually aimed at debilitating the authority of the Senate and consuls, and Cicero, now himself a consul and a staunch supporter of Senatorial authority, speaks in Rabirius's defense. The introduction (exordium) *of the speech, marked by its serious and solemn tone, striking rhetorical figures, amplification, and stately periodic structure, presents a good example of the grand style:*

Although, fellow citizens, it is not customary for me, as I begin speaking, to render an account

of my reasons for defending a particular client—
for I have always considered the perilous situation of any citizen's standing trial a sufficient
reason for my bond with him—nevertheless, in
this, my defense of Gaius Rabirius's life, reputation, and fortunes, it appears necessary to set
forth a rationale of my services to him; for my
reason for defending him, which seems to me to
be most just, should to you seem the same for
acquitting him. To be sure, the longevity of our
friendship, the high standing of my client, the de-
mands of human kindness, and the practice that
I have followed my entire life have urged me to
defend Rabirius; but the welfare of the Republic,
my duty as consul, indeed the consulship itself,
commended to me by you along with the welfare
of the Republic, have compelled me to defend
him most zealously. Certainly it is not the guilt
attached to the charge, nor jealousy of his life,
nor the deep, long-standing, even just enmity
felt by private citizens that has summoned Gaius
Rabirius to court on a capital charge; rather, in
order to remove from the Republic the chief bulwark of its imperial majesty handed down to us
by our ancestors, so that from this point on neither the authority of the Senate, nor the power

of the consuls, nor concord among good citizens would have any potency—for this reason, I say, amid the overturning of these institutions, the old age, the infirmity, and the isolation of this one man have been assailed. If, therefore, it is the mark of a good consul, when he sees all the supports of the Republic shaken and torn apart, to bring aid to the country, to rush to secure the welfare and fortunes of all, to plead for the loyalty of the citizens, and to consider the public welfare before his own; it is also the mark of good and courageous citizens, such as you have shown yourselves in all crises of the Republic, to block all paths to sedition, to fortify the bulwarks of the Republic, to consider that supreme power resides with the consuls, and supreme deliberative power with the Senate, and to judge that he who has adhered to these principles is worthy of praise and honor rather than condemnation and punishment. Wherefore, while the task of defending Rabirius is chiefly mine, eagerness to save him will have to be shared by me along with you.

For you should understand, fellow citizens, that never in human memory has a case more important, more dangerous, more worthy of your caution been undertaken by a tribune of the people or resisted by a consul or referred to the Roman people. For this case is being undertaken, fellow citizens, for no other reason than to ensure that from this day forward there be no general council in the Republic, no concord among good citizens against the fury and audacity of wicked men, no safe haven for the Republic when in dire straits, no bulwark for its welfare. Since this is the situation, I, because duty demands it when engaged in such a monumental struggle on behalf of a man's life, reputation, and all his fortunes, first beg of Jupiter, most high and mighty, and of all the other immortal gods and goddesses to grant peace and favor; and I pray that they have allowed this day to dawn for the purposes both of preserving the welfare of my client and of setting strong the foundations of the Republic. Next I beg and implore you, fellow citizens, whose power most closely approximates the divine will of the immortal gods, since at one and the same time the life of the very hapless and innocent Gaius Rabirius, as well as the welfare of the Republic are entrusted to your hands and to your votes, to apply your accustomed mercy in regard to the fortunes of my client, your accustomed wisdom in regard to the welfare of the Republic. (*Pro Rabirio* 1–5)

Memory

Memory is the fourth part of rhetoric, or activity of the orator. Speakers in our modern world can have recourse to written texts, computer screens, and teleprompters to help them in the delivery of their speech, discourse, or argument. In such an environment, we tend to forget that the ancient orator depended almost entirely upon memory when arguing a point or delivering a speech. Difficulty in manipulating ancient writing materials, the awkwardness of handling scrolls, the expense of written materials and lack of indices, along with an absence of modern audio-visual electronic equipment, made dependence on one's memory a given in Cicero's day. Even though some of the stories about prodigious feats of memory from antiquity might be subject to hyperbole, it is certain that the ancients were called upon to use and exercise their memories to a much greater extent than are we. For example, a speaker of Cicero's ability and reputation could deliver a speech that lasted several hours, all from memory.

Ancient theorists identified two types of memory, natural and artificial. Natural memory is the memory that is embedded in our minds, and simultaneously occurs with our thought. Artificial memory is memory that comes from art or technique, that is, memory that is strengthened by training and discipline; in that connection, an elaborate system of localities and images was developed for the purpose of enhancing artificial memory. In order to recall a series of facts or details, one would choose a familiar location (for example, the houses on your street, or the entranceway to your home), and then link the things to be recalled with the series of localities in sequence. The system could be used for memorizing both words and content, and appears to have been extremely effective. Remarkably, such a system remains at the core of all modern memory systems today.

Despite our ready access to computers and teleprompters, the ability to deliver an argument or speech from memory, recalling pertinent facts without reliance on other means, is an effective tool in oral communication and can certainly enhance any speaker's presentation. In De oratore *(2.351–60), Cicero relates the origin of this type of memory system and outlines the benefits that having a good memory offer to a speaker.*

And I am thankful to Simonides of Ceos, who is said to have been the first to introduce the art of memory. According to this story, Simonides was dining at Crannon in Thessaly at the house of Scopas, a rich nobleman. When he had finished singing the poem that he had composed in Scopas's honor, in which he had written much about Castor and Pollux for the sake of embellishment, as poets do, Scopas reacted with excessive stinginess. He told him that he would pay him only half the agreed fee for this poem; if he liked, he could ask for the rest from his friends Castor and Pollux, who had received half the praise. A little later, the story goes on, Simonides received a message to go outside: two young men were standing at the door, who were urgently asking for him. He got up and went outside, but saw no one. In the meantime, precisely while he was gone, the room where Scopas was giving his banquet collapsed, and Scopas, together with his relatives, was buried under the fallen roof and died. When their families wanted to arrange their funerals, but could not possibly distinguish them because they had been completely crushed, it was reportedly Simonides who, from his recollection of the place where each of them had been reclining at table, identified every one of them for burial. Prompted by this experience, he is then said to have made the discovery that order is what most brings light to our memory. And he concluded that those who would like to employ this part of their abilities should choose localities, then form mental images of the things they wanted to store in their memory, and place these in the localities. In this way, the order of the localities would preserve the order of the things, while the images would represent the things themselves; and we would use the localities like a wax tablet, and the representations like the letters written on it.

What need is there for me to mention the benefit that the memory offers to the orator, its great usefulness and its great power? That you can retain what you learned when accepting a case, as well as what you have thought out yourself about it? That you can have all of your thoughts fixed in your mind, and your entire supply of words neatly arranged? That you can listen in such a way to your client who instructs you about the case, or to your opponent whom you will have to answer, that what they say is not just poured into your ears, but seems inscribed into your mind? Accordingly, only those with a powerful memory know what they are going to say, how far they will pursue it, how they will say it, which points they have already answered and which still remain. Such people also remember much of the material they have used in the past in other cases, and much that they have heard others use. Now I do acknowledge that nature is the chief source of this asset, as it is of everything that I have been talking about before. But it is true of the whole art of speaking, . . . that its function is not to produce or create from scratch what is nowhere present in our own natural abilities, but to rear and develop what has already been born and created within us. Yet, there is barely anyone whose memory is so keen that he can retain the order of all words and thoughts without arranging his material and representing it by symbols; nor anyone, really, whose memory is so dull that practicing this system on a regular basis will not help him at all.

Indeed, as Simonides wisely observed—or whoever it was who discovered this—the things best pictured by our minds are those that have been conveyed and imprinted on them by one of the senses. Now the keenest of all our senses is the sense of sight. Therefore, things perceived by our hearing or during our thought processes can be most easily grasped by the mind if they are also conveyed to our minds through the mediation of the eyes. In this way, as he saw, invisible objects that are inaccessible to the judgment of sight are represented by a kind of figure, an image, a shape, so that things we can scarcely take hold of by thinking may be grasped, so to speak, by looking at them. But these concrete forms, just like everything that falls under the faculty of sight, must be located somewhere, for a concrete object without a locality is inconceivable. Consequently (for I don't want to talk too much or be obtrusive while the subject is so well-known and common), the localities we use must be numerous, clearly visible, and at moderate intervals, while our images should be lively, sharp, and conspicuous, with the potential to present themselves quickly and to strike the mind. Practice, the starting point for developing a habit, will provide the requisite skill. . . . Memorization of words, which is less necessary for us, is characterized by a greater variety of images. After all, there are many words that serve as joints connecting the limbs of our language, and it is impossible to find shapes that resemble these. For them, we must mold images for constant use. Memorization of content, however, is the proper business of the orator. This is where we can use representation by separate, well-placed persons and objects, so that we can apprehend thoughts by means of images, and their order by means of the localities.

And it is not true, as lazy people always say, that the memory is overwhelmed by the weight of the images, and that they even obscure what our natural memory could have grasped by itself. I myself have met eminent people with almost superhuman memories, Charmadas in Athens and in Asia Metrodorus of Scepsis (who is said to be still alive); and both said that they recorded what they wanted to remember by means of images in the localities that they had chosen, just as if they were writing them out by means of letters on a wax tablet. Hence, if someone does not have a natural faculty of memory, this practice cannot be used to unearth one, but if one is latent, the practice should be used to make it grow.

Delivery

We have all probably heard the old adage, "It's not what you say, but how you say it," and we know from the experience of listening to public speakers —be they politicians, priests, or professors—that there is much truth in that statement. At times this can be a very unfortunate circumstance, for example, when a very good message with very important content is obscured because of a terrible presentation; or conversely, when poor content, or even false and misleading information is made to sound appealing and overwhelmingly convincing because of an excellent manner of presentation. In any case, the importance of delivery, the fifth and final activity of the orator, was highly appreciated in antiquity, just as it is today. In fact, in order to illustrate its importance, Cicero was wont to relate a famous anecdote about the great Greek orator, Demosthenes:

. . . and this bears out the truth of the saying attributed to Demosthenes, who, when asked what was the primary consideration in speaking, replied "delivery"; what was second, "delivery"; and again, what was third, "delivery." No other thing penetrates the mind more deeply, fashions, forms, and flexes it, and causes speakers to seem such persons as they themselves wish to seem. (*Brutus* 142)

So, just as "location, location, location" is a prime factor in real estate considerations, so is delivery in terms of argument and oratory. Theoretical discussions of delivery often divided the subject into two categories, voice and movement, with movement then further subdivided into gesture and facial expression. In De oratore, *Cicero discusses voice, gesture, and facial expression, and links them closely to portraying the emotions desired by the speaker. In the following passage, Crassus, the chief character of the dialogue, discusses these topics with the others and relates other interesting anecdotes about the delivery of skillful speakers:*

All of these things, however, are as effective as their delivery makes them. Delivery, I am telling you, is the one dominant factor in oratory. Without it, even the best orator cannot be of any account at all, while an average speaker equipped with this skill can often outdo the best orators. It is to delivery that they say Demosthenes, when asked what was most important in oratory, gave first, second, and third place. And I generally tend to think that what Aeschines said is even better. Having been disgracefully defeated in court, he had left Athens and taken refuge at Rhodes. There, he is said to have read, at the request of the Rhodians, the outstanding speech that he had given against Ctesiphon, when Demosthenes was pleading for the defense. After completing the reading, he was also asked to read, on the next day, the speech that Demosthenes had delivered on the other side, on behalf of Ctesiphon. This he did in an extremely powerful and pleasant voice, and when everyone expressed admiration, he said, "How much more you would admire it, if you had heard Demosthenes himself!" By this comment, he sufficiently indicated the great importance of delivery, inasmuch as in his view, the same speech would actually be different if someone else were to deliver it. What was it in Gracchus, whom you, Catulus, remember better than I, that was talked about so much when I was young? "Where can I take refuge in my misery? Where can I turn? To the Capitol? But that is overflowing with my brother's blood!

To home? So that I can see my mother in misery, grief-stricken and downcast?" People generally agreed that, when delivering these words, he used his eyes, voice, and gestures to such effect that even his enemies could not contain their tears. I am talking about this in some detail because the orators, who act in real life, have abandoned this entire field, while the actors, who are only imitators of reality, have appropriated it. And no doubt, in everything reality has the advantage over imitation. Yet if reality by itself were sufficiently effective in delivery, we would have no need for any art at all. But emotions, which must especially be expressed or imitated through delivery, are often so confused that they are obscured and almost smothered. So we must get rid of what obscures them and embrace their most prominent and most clearly visible features. For by nature, every emotion has its own facial expression, tone of voice, and gesture. The entire body of a human being, all the facial expressions and all the utterances of the voice, like the strings on a lyre, "sound" exactly in the way they are struck by each emotion.

The voice is stretched taut like the strings of an instrument, to respond to each and every touch, to sound high, low, fast, slow, loud, and soft. And apart from each of these extremes, there is also, in each category, a middle between the extremes. Moreover, from these kinds of sounds are also derived others: smooth and rough, restrained and wide-ranging, sustained and staccato, hoarse and cracked, and with crescendo and diminuendo and a changing of pitch. The employment of each of these kinds falls under the regulation of art. They are at our disposal to be varied at will in delivery, just as colors are in painting. Anger requires the use of one kind of voice, high and sharp, excited, breaking off repeatedly. . . . Fear again has another kind of voice, subdued, hesitating, and downcast. . . . Energy has yet another kind, intense, vehement, threatening, and with an earnest sort of excitement. . . .

Happiness needs another tone, unrestrained and tender, cheerful and relaxed. . . .

All of these emotions ought to be accompanied by gestures—not those used in the manner of the stage, which depict the individual words, but gestures that indicate the content and the ideas as a whole, not by imitating them, but by signifying them. For this, one needs the vigorous and manly attitude of the body derived not from stage-actors, but from those who fight with weapons or in the palaestra. The hands should not be too expressive, accompanying rather than depicting the words with the fingers. The arm should extend forward a bit, as if our speech were employing it as a weapon. And you should stamp your foot at the beginning or at the end of energetic passages.

But everything depends on the face; and this, in turn, is entirely dominated by the eyes. So the older generation was quite right to praise not even Roscius overmuch when he acted wearing a mask. For delivery is wholly a matter of the soul, and the face is an image of the soul, while the eyes reflect it. The face is the only part of the body that can produce as many varying signs as there are feelings in the soul; and there is surely no one who could produce these same effects with his eyes closed. Theophrastus actually says that a certain Tauriscus was fond of calling someone who fixed his eyes on some object while delivering his speech "an actor with his back turned." Consequently, it is quite important to regulate the expression of the eyes. We should not alter the appearance of the face itself too much, so as to avoid distorting it or acting like a fool. It is the eyes that should be used to signify our feelings in a way suited to the actual type of our speech, by an intense or relaxed, or a fixed or cheerful look. Delivery is, so to speak, the language of the body, which makes it all the more essential that it should correspond to what we intend to say; and nature has actually given us eyes, as it has given the horse and the lion their manes, tails, and ears, for indicating our feelings. So the most effective element in our delivery, next to the voice, is the expression on our face; and this is controlled by our eyes.

Now all the elements of delivery possess a certain force that has been bestowed by nature. That is why delivery strongly affects even the inexperienced, the common crowd, and also foreigners. After all, words affect only those who are joined to the speaker by the bond of a shared language, and clever thoughts often escape the understanding of people who are not so clever. But delivery, which displays the feelings of the soul, affects everyone, because everyone's soul is stirred by the same feelings, and it is through the same signs that people recognize them in others and reveal them in themselves.

When we look at effectiveness and excellence in delivery, the voice undoubtedly plays the most important part. In the first place, a good voice is a desirable thing to have; but in the second place, whatever sort of voice we do have, it is something that ought to be protected. In this connection, the question of how to care for our voice is not really pertinent to the kind of instruction I am giving now (though I do believe that we should take good care of it). But the observation that I made a little while ago seems not at all irrelevant to my task in this conversation, namely that in the majority of things, what is most useful is somehow also what is most appropriate. In order to preserve the voice, nothing is more useful than frequent modulation, while nothing is more harmful than unrestrained, uninterrupted exertion. And indeed, what is more suitable for our ears and for a pleasing delivery than alternation, variety, and change? Actually, the Gracchus whom I mentioned earlier acted accordingly. . . . When he was addressing a public meeting, he always had someone standing inconspicuously behind him with a little ivory flute, a skillful man who would sound a quick note that would either rouse him when his voice had dropped, or call him back when he was speaking in a strained voice. . . . There is a middle range in every voice (though this is different in every individual case). Raising the voice gradually from this level is useful as well as pleasing, since shouting right from the start is a coarse thing to do, and this gradual approach is at the same time salutary, as it will strengthen the voice. Moreover, there is a certain limit to raising the voice (which is still below the level of shouting at the highest pitch). Beyond this the flute will not allow you to go, while it will also call you back when you are actually reaching this limit. Likewise, at the other end of the scale, when you are dropping your voice there is also a lowest sound, and this you reach step by step, descending from pitch to pitch. By this variation, and by thus running through all the pitches, the voice will both preserve itself and make the delivery pleasing. And while you will leave the man with his flute at home, you will bring with you to the forum a feeling for these things, derived from practice. (*De oratore* 3.213–27)

THE VALUE OF IMITATING
GOOD MODELS OF SPEAKING

In antiquity as today, the imitation of good models was considered an effective means of educa-

tion. In fact, in Cicero's day it was common for a young man to enter into a sort of apprenticeship, called the tirocinium fori, *during which he would be attached to a prominent citizen or statesmen in order to observe his activity in the forum and in the courts. It was also important to choose good models in public speaking, and to imitate their strengths, while disregarding their weaknesses. Antonius, the other chief character in* De oratore, *expounds on the use of good models of effective persuasion, as he gives advice to his young protégés, Catulus and Sulpicius, on this matter:*

Well, Catulus, let me take our friend Sulpicius here as my starting point: I first heard him in a minor case, when he was quite young. His voice, his appearance, his bodily movements, and all his other qualities were well-suited for the task that we are considering. His manner of speaking, however, was quick and impetuous—a mark of his talent; his words were boiling over with excitement and were a little too exuberant—a mark of his youth. I did not think this contemptible: I like to see fertility in a young man. For, as with vines, it is easier to check what has grown too abundantly than to produce new shoots by cultivation if the stock is weak. Likewise, in a young man, I want to have something to prune away. For in a growth that has reached maturity too quickly, vitality cannot be long-lived. I immediately recognized his talent, and without losing any time, I encouraged him to take the forum as the school where he could learn, and to choose the teacher he preferred—but if he listened to my advice, it should be Lucius Crassus. The fellow jumped at my suggestion and assured me that this was what he was going to do, also adding, out of courtesy no doubt, that I too would be his teacher. Scarcely a year had passed from the time of the conversation in which I gave him this encouragement when he prosecuted Gaius Norbanus and I defended him. The difference that I noticed between the Sulpicius of that occasion and the one that I had seen the year before was incredible. It is absolutely true that his own natural abilities were leading him to that magnificent and splendid manner of Crassus. This would not, however, have enabled him to achieve sufficient results, had he not aimed at this same goal by energetically imitating Crassus and developed the habit of speaking with all his thoughts and attention focused on him.

This, then, must be the first rule I give to the prospective orator: I will show him whom he should imitate. The next thing, to be joined to this, is practice, through which he must imitate and thus carefully reproduce his chosen model, but not in the way I have known many imitators to do. For people often direct their imitation to features that are easily copied, or even to all but faulty ones that happen to be conspicuous. Nothing is easier than to imitate the way someone dresses or stands or moves. And surely if the model has some fault, it is no great thing to adopt that and to exhibit the same fault yourself, like this Fufius, who is raving on in the State even now, after losing his voice. His oratory fails to achieve the vigor of Gaius Fimbria (which the latter certainly possessed), while he does imitate his distorted mouth and his broad pronunciation. But Fufius did not know how to choose the most suitable model for himself, and the model he did choose, he wanted to imitate even in terms of his faults. Anyone who is going to do things properly must, first, be very careful in making his choice; and he must also devote all his attention to attaining those qualities of his approved model that are truly outstanding. . . .

Whoever, then, wants to achieve such resemblance through imitation, must pursue this goal by frequent and extensive practice, and particularly by writing. Our friend Sulpicius's language would be much more compact, if he did this; as it is, it occasionally has a sort of luxuriance about it (as farmers say about grass when it is at the height of its growth), which should be grazed down by the pen. (*De oratore* 2.88–92, 96)

THE VALUE OF WRITING TO PREPARE FOR EFFECTIVE SPEAKING

The importance of learning to write clearly and cogently is well recognized in educational circles today. Increasing numbers, too, are acknowledging the importance of effective verbal communication as an important skill to be imparted to our students entering the world. The link between good speaking and good writing, while not readily apparent to some, was certainly clear to Cicero. As mentioned earlier (12–13), effective written composition entails the activities of invention, arrangement, and style—the first three of the five activities of the orator, and as such serves as a model exercise in training for effective speaking.

For my part, said Crassus, I approve of your habit of taking as a starting point some case very similar to those brought into the forum, and of speaking on it in a manner that is as true to life as possible. Most people, however, when doing this, merely exercise their voices (and not very knowledgeably at that), build their strength, quicken the speed of their tongues, and revel in the flood of their words. They have heard the saying that the way to become a speaker is to speak, and this misleads them. For there is another saying that is equally true: the easiest way to become a wretched speaker is to speak wretchedly. For this reason, although it is also useful, in these practice sessions of yours, to speak extemporaneously on a regular basis, it is still more useful to take some time for reflection, in order to speak better prepared and with greater care.

What is most fundamental, however, is something that, to be honest, we do least of all (for it involves a great deal of effort, which most of us try to avoid)—I mean writing as much as possible. It is the pen, the pen, that is the best and most eminent teacher and creator of speaking. And I am saying this with very good reason: if extemporaneous and random speech is easily surpassed by preparation and reflection, the latter, in turn, will certainly be outdone by constant and diligent writing. For as we investigate the matter and consider it with all of our powers of discernment, all commonplaces (at least as far as they are inherent in the subject on which we are writing), those provided by the art as well as those provided, in a way, by natural ability and intelligence, occur to us, revealing themselves to our minds. All the thoughts and all the words that are most appropriate to each type of subject, and that are most clear and brilliant, cannot help but pass under the point of our pen one after the other. In addition, writing perfects the ability of actually arranging and combining words, not in a poetic, but in a kind of oratorical measure and rhythm. These are the things that win a good orator shouts of approval and admiration, and no one will master them unless he has written long and written much—even if he has trained himself ever so vigorously in those extemporaneous speeches. Also, whoever comes to oratory after much practice in writing brings this ability along: even when he is improvising, what he says will still turn out to resemble a written text. And what is more, should he take a piece of text with him when he is going to speak, once he has stopped following this, the remainder of his speech will continue to resemble it. A ship at full speed, when once the rowers rest upon their oars, still maintains its own momentum and course, even though the thrust of the oar strokes has been interrupted. The same thing happens in the case of a speech: when the written text leaves off, the remainder of the speech still maintains a like course, sped on by the similarity to what was written and by its impulse.

What I used to do as a very young man in my daily practice sessions was to apply myself especially to the same exercise that I knew Gaius Carbo, my old enemy, had always employed. I would set up as a model some verses, as impressive as possible, or I would read a speech, as much of it as I could manage to memorize, and then I would express exactly what I had read, choosing different words as much as I could. But after a while, I noticed this method had a defect: the words that were most fitting in each case, and that were the finest and most distinguished, had already been appropriated by Ennius (if I was practicing with his verses) or by Gracchus (if I happened to use a speech of his as my model). If, therefore, I chose the same words, I gained nothing, and if I chose others, I was actually doing myself harm, because I was getting used to employing words that were less appropriate. Afterward, it seemed a good idea—and this was the practice I adopted when I was a bit older—to take speeches of the great orators from Greece and reformulate them. The advantage of choosing these was not only that, when rendering in Latin what I had read in Greek, I could use the finest words that were nevertheless common, but also that, by imitating Greek words, I could coin certain others that were new to our language—provided they were appropriate. (*De oratore* 1.149–55)

THE REQUIREMENTS AND EDUCATION OF THE IDEAL SPEAKER

As we look back on the entries in this brief volume, and consider the activities of the speaker and rhetorical precepts offered in the typical rhetorical handbooks of Cicero's day, we realize that we have encountered only the proverbial tip of the iceberg; a full accounting of all the rules for persuasion would fill many volumes of this size.

Moreover, according to Cicero, the precepts for persuasion contained in the typical handbooks are only a small part of what goes into creating a real speaker, one who possesses the genuine power and ability to persuade his listeners. The challenge of speaking effectively in public is a monumental one, and to do so with effectiveness and success requires not merely knowledge of the precepts of the art of rhetoric, a considerable amount of inborn talent, and diligent practice, but also a capacious knowledge, broad and deep, of those subjects that we still know today as the "liberal arts." It is fitting to conclude our survey of Ciceronian persuasion where Cicero himself begins—in the preface of De oratore, addressed to his brother, Quintus, Marcus speaks at some length about the difficulty of becoming a great speaker, and he outlines what he considers the requisites of the "ideal" orator, the exploration of which he then pursues in the subsequent pages of his great masterpiece. As he readily concedes, few people are up to such demands, but knowledge of the art, application of our intellects, and a broad education will help all of us to become more effective speakers, who know how to convince people and win an argument.

For my part, whenever I reflect upon the greatest and most gifted men, it always seems that the following question requires an answer: why have more people come forward to distinguish themselves in every other art than in oratory? Turn your thoughts and attention where you will, and you see a great many who excel in each kind of endeavor—not merely in the minor arts, but in those we might call the most important. For instance, should anyone choose to evaluate the knowledge of illustrious men in terms of the usefulness or importance of their accomplishments, would he not grant precedence to the general over the orator? Yet there is no doubt that, even from our State alone, we could produce an almost endless list of absolutely outstanding leaders in war, but could name barely a few who have excelled in oratory. Furthermore, many have emerged who had the ability to guide and steer the State by wisdom and counsel—many in our own memory, more in our fathers', and even more in our ancestors'—whereas for quite a long time there were no good speakers at all, and entire generations scarcely produced even a tolerable one.

But some perhaps think that this art of oratory should be compared with other pursuits, namely those involved with abstruse branches of study and with varied and extensive reading, rather than with the qualities of the general or the wisdom of the good senator. If so, let them indeed turn their attention to these kinds of arts and examine who and how many have distinguished themselves in each. In this way, they will quite easily infer how very small the number of orators is and always has been. For instance, as you of course know, the most learned consider philosophy, as the Greeks call it, to be the creator and mother of all the valuable arts, so to speak. Yet even here in philosophy, it is difficult to reckon how many people there have been (so notable for their abundant knowledge and for the variety and vast range of their studies!) who have not only worked as specialists in one single area, but have embraced all that exists in their thorough investigations or their dialectical reasonings. We all know how obscure the subjects handled by the so-called mathematicians are, and how abstruse, complex, and exact is the art with which they deal. Yet even in this area, so many geniuses have emerged that almost no one who has devoted his energies to mastering it appears to have been unsuccessful. As to the theory of music, and the study of language and literature so popular nowadays (the profession of the so-called grammarians)—has anyone really dedicated himself to them without managing to acquire enough knowledge to cover the complete, almost infinite range and material of those arts? I think I am justified in saying that, of all those who have been involved in the pursuit and study of the truly noble arts, the smallest contingent to emerge has been that of outstanding poets and speakers. Yet again, if you look at this group, where excellence is so very rare, and are willing to make a careful selection both from our number and from that of the Greeks, you will find that there have been far fewer good orators than good poets.

This fact is all the more amazing when we realize that the study of the other arts draws as a rule upon abstruse and hidden sources, whereas all the procedures of oratory lie within everyone's reach, and are concerned with everyday experience and with human nature and speech. This means that in the other arts the highest achievement is precisely that which is most remote from what the uninitiated can understand and perceive, whereas in oratory it is the worst possible fault to deviate from the ordinary mode of speaking and the generally accepted way of looking at things. One cannot even truly maintain that more people dedicate themselves to the other arts, or that those who do are motivated to master them because these offer more pleasure or richer hopes or greater rewards. And in this respect, I need not mention Greece, which has always aspired to the leading position in eloquence, or the famous city of Athens, the inventor of all learning, where oratory in its highest form was both discovered and perfected, for surely even in this community of ours, no study has ever enjoyed more vigorous popularity than the study of eloquence. Once we had established our authority over all nations and a stable peace had provided us with leisure, almost every ambitious young man thought he should devote himself to oratory with all the energy he had. At first, it is true, they accomplished only as much as their own natural ability and reflection allowed, for they were unaware of any theory, and assumed there was no definite method of practicing or any rule of art whatsoever. But once they had heard Greek orators, had come to know Greek writings on the subject, and had called in teachers, our people were fired with a really incredible zeal for learning all these things. They were urged on by the scope, variety, and frequency of cases of every type, so that the theoretical knowledge that each had acquired by his own study was supplemented by constant practice, which was more effective than the precepts of all teachers. In addition, there were laid before them, just as there are now, the greatest rewards for this pursuit, in terms of influence, power, and prestige. Moreover, there are many indications that the natural ability of our people was far superior to that of all others, from every other nation.

Considering all this, who would not rightly be amazed that, in the entire history of generations, of ages, and of communities, such a slight number of orators is to be found? The truth of the matter is, however, that this faculty is something greater, and is a combination of more arts and pursuits, than is generally supposed. For, in view of the enormous number of apprentices, the rich supply of available teachers, the exceptional talents engaged, the infinite variety of cases, and the utterly magnificent rewards held out for eloquence, the only conceivable explanation of this scarcity is surely the incredible scope and difficulty of oratory. To begin with, one must acquire knowledge of a very great number of things, for without this a ready flow of words is empty and ridiculous; the language itself has to be shaped, not only by the choice of words but by their arrangement as well; also required is a thorough acquaintance with all the emotions with which nature has endowed the human race, because in soothing or in exciting the feelings of the audience the full force of oratory and all its available means must be brought into play. In addition, it is essential to possess a certain esprit and humor, the culture that befits a gentleman, and an ability to be quick and concise in rebuttal as well as attack, combined with refinement, grace, and urbanity. Moreover, one must know the whole past with its storehouse of examples and precedents, nor should one fail to master statutes and the civil law. Surely I don't need to add anything about delivery? This must be regulated by the movement of the body, by gesture, by facial expression, and by inflecting and varying the voice. Just how much effort this requires, even by itself, is indicated by the trivial art of actors on the stage. For although every one of them strives to regulate his facial expression, voice, and movement, we all know how really few actors there are, and have been, whom we can watch without irritation. What shall I say about that universal treasure-house, the memory? It is clear that unless this faculty is applied as a guard over the ideas and words that we have devised and thought out for our speech, all the qualities of the orator, however brilliant, will go to waste.

Let us stop wondering, then, why there are so few eloquent speakers, seeing that eloquence depends on the combination of all these accomplishments, any one of which alone would be a tremendous task to perfect. Let us rather encourage our children, and all others whose fame and reputation are dear to us, to appreciate fully its enormous scope. They should not rely on the precepts or the teachers or the methods of practice in general use, but be confident that they can achieve their goals by means that are of a quite different order. It is at least my opinion that it will be impossible for anyone to be an orator endowed with all praiseworthy qualities, unless he has gained a knowledge of all important subjects and arts. For it is certainly from knowledge that a speech should blossom and acquire fullness: unless the orator has firmly grasped the underlying subject matter, his speech will remain an utterly empty, yes, almost childish verbal exercise. (*De oratore* 1.6–20)

A CICERONIAN CHEAT SHEET FOR EFFECTIVE SPEAKING

1. *Nature, art, and practice, practice, practice.* These are the three requisites for becoming an effective speaker. The good speaker must possess certain qualities bestowed by nature, for example, a pleasant voice and the ability to project it. Knowledge of the systematic body of rhetorical precepts, that is, mastery of the "art" of rhetoric, is likewise essential. Finally, one's natural gifts and knowledge of the rules must be polished and enhanced by diligent and purposeful practice.

2. *Eloquence is a powerful weapon.* The human capacity for thought and the ability to express that thought through persuasive speech are, according to Cicero, what separate humans from all other creatures. When channeled correctly and informed by good thinking, eloquent speech is the most powerful weapon

for effecting good in society. The most gifted speakers should always keep in mind the power that their speech wields over others, and use it for the betterment of their communities.

3. *Identify, arrange, memorize.* When setting out to construct an argument or a speech, one should first identify the point at issue and discover appropriate material for proving it; next, arrange that material effectively and strategically; apply a fitting style; then (if necessary) commit it to memory; and finally, employ appropriate ways to deliver the argument(s). These are the so-called activities of a speaker, outlining the tasks and the order in which to construct an effective speech. The first three activities can also be employed effectively in written composition.

4. *Not by logic alone.* Persuasion involves more than simply arguing logically. The speaker has available three sources of persuasion: rational argumentation, proof based on character, and emotional appeal. Aristotle identified these sources of proof or persuasion, and Cicero recommends using all of them—to teach, to delight, and to move our audience. One can argue using the tools of

logic, for example, deductive and inductive reasoning as illustrated by the syllogism and example; or rely on proof based in the portrayal of one's character; or persuade by appealing to the emotions. There are times and places for each, and the skillful speaker will know when and where to engage these various modes of proof.

5. *Know your audience.* When actually composing the words, sentences, and paragraphs of an argument or a speech, the speaker should remember that different styles exist, and that a particular occasion and audience demand a particular and suitable style, be it the plain, middle, or grand. It makes a difference whether one is arguing with a friend, or presenting a position paper in a class, or arguing a brief before a court of law. The effective speaker will adapt his or her level of style according to the occasion and the audience that is being addressed.

6. *Be clear, be correct.* Regardless of the particular style adopted, speakers will assiduously apply the "virtues," or qualities of style, to their speech or argument: correctness, clarity, distinction, and appropriateness. No matter

the stylistic level at which an argument is pitched, the speaker must ensure that the language employed is correct in its syntax and grammar, that it is expressed in the clearest possible way, that it is made distinctive by the use of figures of thought and speech, and that it is entirely appropriate to the time, occasion, and audience.

7. *Delivery matters.* Sometimes it's not what you say, but how you say it. Cicero understood and appreciated the power of delivery, that is, the way a speech or argument is presented. All of us, perhaps, have experienced a teacher who was in possession of a brilliant intellect and encyclopedic knowledge of a subject, but could not present that material clearly and cogently; conversely, we have perhaps also heard a politician or a salesman sweep people off their feet with a dazzling presentation that, under closer inspection, lacks any real substance. Effective delivery of an argument or a speech, employing both voice and gesture skillfully, can be the decisive factor in winning an argument.

8. *Imitation is the sincerest form of flattery— and more.* Cicero believed strongly in find-

ing good models to imitate. The best speakers are those who have identified excellent models and who have made it a habit to imitate their strengths, while leaving aside their weaknesses. Several models are worthy of consideration, gleaning what is best from each.

9. *The pen is often mightier than the sword.* The tongue may be a gifted speaker's most important weapon, but the pen, according to Cicero, is close behind. If you wish to improve your speaking ability, writing— and writing variously and much—is, Cicero maintains, the key to achieving your goal.

10. *Words, without substance, are hollow things.* Cicero believed firmly that the most effective, persuasive speech follows naturally from the underlying subject matter. Without solid and extensive knowledge as a foundation, the words that flow from a speaker's mouth are nothing but child's prattle. For this reason, Cicero's ideal speaker is one who not only knows and understands the rules as outlined in the "art" of rhetoric, but even more importantly is a person who is steeped in the knowledge of literature, history, law,

philosophy—in short, in all of those subjects we know today as the "liberal arts." As an earlier Roman, Cato the Elder, was fond of saying, *rem tene, verba sequentur* ("grasp the subject, the words will follow").

LATIN TEXTS

The Origins of Eloquent and Persuasive Speech

Nature, Art, Practice

De inventione 1.2–3: Ac si volumus huius rei quae vocatur eloquentia, sive artis sive studi sive exercitationis cuiusdam sive facultatis ab natura profectae considerare principium, reperiemus id ex honestissimis causis natum atque optimis rationibus profectum. Nam fuit quoddam tempus cum in agris homines passim bestiarum modo vagabantur et sibi victu fero vitam propagabant, nec ratione animi quicquam, sed pleraque viribus corporis administrabant; nondum divinae religionis, non humani offici ratio colebatur, nemo nuptias viderat legitimas, non certos quisquam aspexerat liberos, non, ius aequabile quid utilitatis haberet, acceperat. Ita propter errorem atque inscientiam caeca ac temeraria dominatrix animi cupiditas ad se explendam viribus corporis abutebatur, perniciosissimis satellitibus.

Quo tempore quidam magnus videlicet vir et sapiens cognovit quae materia esset et quanta ad maximas res opportunitas in animis inesset hominum, si quis eam posset elicere et praecipiendo meliorem reddere; qui dispersos homines in agros et in tectis silvestribus abditos ratione quadam compulit unum in locum et congregavit et eos in unam quamque rem inducens utilem atque honestam primo propter insolentiam reclamantes, deinde propter rationem atque orationem studiosius audientes ex feris et immanibus mites reddidit et mansuetos.

Ac mihi quidem videtur hoc nec tacita nec inops dicendi sapientia perficere potuisse ut homines a consuetudine subito converteret et ad diversas rationes vitae traduceret. Age vero, urbibus constitutis, ut fidem colere et iustitiam retinere discerent et aliis parere sua voluntate consuescerent ac non modo labores excipiendos communis commodi causa, sed etiam vitam amittendam existimarent, qui tandem fieri potuit, nisi homines ea quae ratione invenissent eloquentia persuadere potuissent? Profecto nemo nisi gravi ac suavi commotus oratione, cum vir-

ibus plurimum posset, ad ius voluisset sine vi
descendere, ut inter quos posset excellere, cum
eis se pateretur aequari et sua voluntate a iucun-
dissima consuetudine recederet quae praesertim
iam naturae vim obtineret propter vetustatem.

Ac primo quidem sic et nata et progressa lon-
gius eloquentia videtur et item postea maximis in
rebus pacis et belli cum summis hominum utili-
tatibus esse versata.

De oratore 1.30–34: . . . neque vero mihi quicquam, inquit, praestabilius videtur quam posse
dicendo tenere hominum mentes, adlicere vol-
untates, impellere quo velit, unde autem velit
deducere. haec una res in omni libero populo
maximeque in pacatis tranquillisque civitatibus
praecipue semper floruit semperque dominata
est. quid enim est aut tam admirabile quam ex
infinita multitudine hominum exsistere unum,
qui id quod omnibus natura sit datum vel solus
vel cum perpaucis facere possit? aut tam iucun-
dum cognitu atque auditu quam sapientibus
sententiis gravibusque verbis ornata oratio et polita? aut tam potens tamque magnificum quam
populi motus iudicum religiones senatus gravitatem unius oratione converti? quid tam porro

regium tam liberale tam munificum quam opem
ferre supplicibus, excitare afflictos, dare salutem,
liberare periculis, retinere homines in civitate?
quid autem tam necessarium quam tenere semper arma, quibus vel tectus ipse esse possis vel
provocare improbos vel te ulcisci lacessitus? age
vero ne semper forum subsellia rostra curiam-
que meditere, quid esse potest in otio aut iu-
cundius aut magis proprium humanitatis quam
sermo facetus ac nulla in re rudis? hoc enim uno
praestamus vel maxime feris, quod conloquimur
inter nos et quod exprimere dicendo sensa possumus. quam ob rem quis hoc non iure miretur
summeque in eo elaborandum esse arbitretur, ut
quo uno homines maxime bestiis praestent in
hoc hominibus ipsis antecellat? ut vero iam ad
illa summa veniamus, quae vis alia potuit aut dispersos homines unum in locum congregare aut
a fera agrestique vita ad hunc humanum cultum
civilemque deducere aut iam constitutis civitatibus leges iudicia iura describere? ac ne plura quae
sunt paene innumerabilia consecter, compre-
hendam brevi: sic enim statuo, perfecti oratoris
moderatione et sapientia non solum ipsius dignitatem sed et privatorum plurimorum et univer-
sae rei publicae salutem maxime contineri. quam

ob rem pergite ut facitis, adulescentes, atque in id studium in quo estis incumbite, ut et vobis honori et amicis utilitati et rei publicae emolumento esse possitis.

De oratore 2.232: observatio quaedam est, ut ipse dixit, earum rerum quae in dicendo valent; quae si eloquentis facere posset, quis esset non eloquens? quis enim haec non vel facile vel certe aliquo modo posset ediscere? sed ego in his praeceptis hanc vim et hanc utilitatem esse arbitror, non ut ad reperiendum quid dicamus arte ducamur, sed ut ea, quae natura, quae studio, quae exercitatione consequimur, aut recta esse confidamus aut prava intellegamus, cum quo referenda sint didicerimus.

Rhetoric and Truth

De inventione 1.1: Saepe et multum hoc mecum cogitavi, bonine an mali plus attulerit hominibus et civitatibus copia dicendi ac summum eloquentiae studium. Nam cum et nostrae rei publicae detrimenta considero et maximarum civitatum veteres animo calamitates colligo, non minimam video per disertissimos homines invectam partem incommodorum; cum autem res ab nostra

memoria propter vetustatem remotas ex litterarum monumentis repetere instituo, multas
urbes constitutas, plurima bella restincta, firmis-
simas societates, sanctissimas amicitias intellego
cum animi ratione tum facilius eloquentia com-
paratas. Ac me quidem diu cogitantem ratio ipsa
in hanc potissimum sententiam ducit, ut existi-
mem sapientiam sine eloquentia parum prodesse
civitatibus, eloquentiam vero sine sapientia nimium
obesse plerumque, prodesse nunquam. Quare si
quis omissis rectissimis atque honestissimis studiis rationis et offici consumit omnem operam
in exercitatione dicendi, is inutilis sibi, perni-
ciosus patriae civis alitur; qui vero ita sese armat
eloquentia, ut non oppugnare commoda patriae,
sed pro his propugnare possit, is mihi vir et suis
et publicis rationibus utilissimus atque amicissi-
mus civis fore videtur.

De officiis 2.51: Atque etiam hoc praeceptum of-
ficii diligenter tenendum est, ne quem umquam
innocentem iudicio capitis arcessas; id enim sine
scelere fieri nullo pacto potest. Nam quid est tam
inhumanum quam eloquentiam a natura ad salutem hominum et ad conservationem datam ad
bonorum pestem perniciemque convertere? Nec

tamen, ut hoc fugiendum est, item est habendum religioni nocentem aliquando, modo ne nefarium impiumque, defendere. Vult hoc multitudo, patitur consuetudo, fert etiam humanitas. Iudicis est semper in causis verum sequi, patroni nonnumquam veri simile, etiam si minus sit verum, defendere.

THE PARTS OF RHETORIC, OR ACTIVITIES OF THE ORATOR

Invention: Identifying and Classifying the Question at Issue According to the Stance of Argument, and Discovering the Sources of Proof

Status *(Stances of Argument)*

De inventione 1.10: Omnis res quae habet in se positam in dictione ac disceptatione aliquam controversiam, aut facti aut nominis aut generis aut actionis continet quaestionem. Eam igitur quaestionem ex qua causa nascitur constitutionem appellamus. Constitutio est prima conflictio causarum ex depulsione intentionis profecta, hoc modo: "Fecisti." "Non feci," aut:

"Iure feci." Cum facti controversia est, quoniam coniecturis causa firmatur, constitutio coniecturalis appellatur. Cum autem nominis, quia vis vocabuli definienda verbis est, constitutio definitiva nominatur. Cum vero qualis res sit quaeritur, quia et de vi et de genere negoti controversia est, constitutio generalis vocatur. At cum causa ex eo pendet, quia non aut is agere videtur quem oportet, aut non cum eo quicum oportet, aut non apud quos, quo tempore, qua lege, quo crimine, qua poena oportet, translativa dicitur constitutio, quia actio translationis et commutationis indigere videtur. Atque harum aliquam in omne causae genus incidere necesse est. Nam in quam rem non inciderit, in ea nihil esse poterit controversiae.

The Sources of Proof

De oratore 2.114–17: Cum igitur acceptae causae et genere cognito rem tractare coepi, nihil prius constituo quam quid sit illud, quo mihi sit referenda omnis illa oratio, quae sit propria quaestionis et iudicii; deinde illa duo diligentissime considero, quorum alterum commendationem habet nostram aut eorum quos defendimus, al-

terum est accommodatum ad eorum animos apud
quos dicimus, ad id quod volumus commovendos. ita omnis ratio dicendi tribus ad persuaden-
dum rebus est nixa: ut probemus vera esse ea quae
defendimus, ut conciliemus eos nobis qui audiunt, ut animos eorum ad quemcumque causa postulabit motum vocemus. ad probandum autem
duplex est oratori subiecta materies: una rerum
earum quae non excogitantur ab oratore, sed
in re positae ratione tractantur, ut tabulae, tes-
timonia, pacta conventa, quaestiones, leges, senatus consulta, res iudicatae, decreta, responsa,
reliqua, si quae sunt, quae non reperiuntur ab
oratore, sed ad oratorem a causa atque a reis
deferuntur; altera est, quae tota in disputatione
et in argumentatione oratoris conlocata est. ita
in superiore genere de tractandis argumentis, in
hoc autem etiam de inveniendis cogitandum est.

De oratore 2.145–47: Huius quidem loci, quem
modo sum exorsus, hic est finis, inquit Antonius—
quoniam intellegeretur non in hominum innu-
merabilibus personis neque in infinita temporum
varietate, sed in generum causis atque naturis
omnia sita esse, quae in dubium vocarentur,

genera autem esse definita non solum numero,
sed etiam paucitate—, ut eam materiem orationis,
quae cuiusque esset generis, studiosi qui essent
dicendi omnibus locis descriptam, instructam or-
natamque comprehenderent, rebus dico et sententiis. ea vi sua verba parient, quae semper satis
ornata mihi quidem videri solent, si eius modi
sunt, ut ea res ipsa peperisse videatur. ac si verum
quaeritis, quod mihi quidem videatur—nihil
enim aliud affirmare possum nisi sententiam et
opinionem meam—hoc instrumentum causarum
et generum universorum in forum deferre debe-
mus neque, ut quaeque res delata ad nos erit,
tum denique scrutari locos, ex quibus argumenta
eruamus, quae quidem omnibus, qui ea mediocriter modo considerarint, studio adhibito et usu
pertractata esse possunt; sed tamen animus ref-
erendus est ad ea capita et ad illos, quos saepe
iam appellavi, locos, ex quibus omnia ad omnem
orationem inventa ducuntur. atque hoc totum
est sive artis sive animadversionis sive consuetudinis nosse regiones, intra quas venere et per-
vestiges, quod quaeras. ubi eum locum omnem
cogitatione saepseris, si modo usu rerum percal-
lueris, nihil te effugiet atque omne, quod erit in
re, occurret atque incidet.

LOGOS (RATIONAL ARGUMENTATION)

De inventione 1.51–52: velut apud Socraticum
Aeschinen demonstrat Socrates cum Xenophontis uxore et cum ipso Xenophonte Aspasiam lo-
cutam: "Dic mihi, quaeso, Xenophontis uxor, si
vicina tua melius habeat aurum quam tu habes,
utrum illudne an tuum malis?" "Illud," inquit.
"Quid si vestem aut ceterum ornatum mulie-
brem preti maioris habeat quam tu habes, tuumne
an illius malis?" Respondit: "Illius vero." "Age
sis," inquit, "quid si virum illa meliorem habeat
quam tu habes, utrumne tuum malis an illius?"
Hic mulier erubuit. Aspasia autem sermonem
cum ipso Xenophonte instituit. "Quaeso," inquit, "Xenophon, si vicinus tuus equum meliorem habeat quam tuus est, tuumne equum
malis an illius?" "Illius," inquit. "Quid si fundum meliorem habeat quam tu habes, utrum
tandem fundum habere malis?" "Illum," inquit,
"meliorem scilicet." "Quid si uxorem meliorem
habeat quam tu habes, utrum tuamne an illius malis?" Atque hic Xenophon quoque ipse
tacuit. Post Aspasia: "Quoniam uterque vestrum," inquit, "id mihi solum non respondit
quod ego solum audire volueram, egomet dicam

quid uterque cogitet. Nam et tu, mulier, opti-
mum virum vis habere et tu, Xenophon, uxorem
habere lectissimam maxime vis. Quare, nisi hoc
perfeceritis, ut neque vir melior neque femina
lectior in terris sit, profecto semper id quod op-
timum putabitis esse, multo maxime requiretis
ut et tu maritus sis quam optimae et haec quam
optimo viro nupta sit." Hic cum rebus non du-
biis assensum est, factum est propter similitudinem, ut etiam illud quod dubium videretur,
si qui separatim quaereret, id pro certo propter
rationem rogandi concederetur.

De inventione 1.58–59: Qui putant in quin-
que tribui partes oportere, aiunt primum con-
venire exponere summam argumentationis, ad
hunc modum: "Melius accurantur quae consilio geruntur quam quae sine consilio administrantur." Hanc primam partem numerant; eam
deinceps rationibus variis et quam copiosissimis
verbis approbari putant oportere, hoc modo:
"Domus ea quae ratione regitur omnibus est
instructior rebus et apparatior quam ea quae te-
mere et nullo consilio administratur. Exercitus is
cui praepositus est sapiens et callidus imperator
omnibus partibus commodius regitur quam is

qui stultitia et temeritate alicuius administratur.
Eadem navigi ratio est. Nam navis optime cursum conficit ea quae scientissimo gubernatore
utitur." Cum propositio sit hoc pacto approbata
et duae partes transierint ratiocinationis, tertia in
parte aiunt, quod ostendere velis, id ex vi prop-
ositionis oportere adsumere, hoc pacto: "Nihil
autem omnium rerum melius, quam omnis mundus, administratur." Huius assumptionis quarto
in loco aliam porro inducunt approbationem,
hoc modo: "Nam et signorum ortus et obitus
definitum quendam ordinem servant et annuae
commutationes non modo quadam ex necessitu-
dine semper eodem modo fiunt, verum ad util-
itates quoque rerum omnium accommodate, et
diurnae nocturnaeque vicissitudines nulla in re
unquam mutatae quicquam nocuerunt." Quae
signo sunt omnia non mediocri quodam consilio
naturam mundi administrari. Quinto inducunt
loco complexionem eam quae aut id infert solum
quod ex omnibus partibus cogitur, hoc modo:
"Consilio igitur mundus administratur," aut
unum in locum cum conduxerit breviter propo-
sitionem et assumptionem, adiungit quid ex his
conficiatur, ad hunc modum: "Quodsi melius
geruntur ea quae consilio quam quae sine consilio

administrantur, nihil autem omnium rerum melius administratur quam omnis mundus, consilio igitur mundus administratur." Quinquepertitam igitur hoc pacto putant esse argumentationem.

ETHOS (ARGUMENT BASED ON CHARACTER)

De oratore 2.182–84: Valet igitur multum ad vincendum probari mores et instituta et facta et vitam eorum, qui agent causas, et eorum pro quibus, et item improbari adversariorum, animosque eorum, apud quos agetur, conciliari quam maxime ad benevolentiam, cum erga oratorem tum erga illum, pro quo dicet orator. conciliantur autem animi dignitate hominis, rebus gestis, existimatione vitae; quae facilius ornari possunt, si modo sunt, quam fingi, si nulla sunt. sed haec adiuvant in oratore lenitas vocis, vultus pudoris significatio, verborum comitas; si quid persequare acrius, ut invitus et coactus facere videare. facilitatis, liberalitatis, mansuetudinis, pietatis, grati animi, non appetentis, non avidi signa proferri perutile est; eaque omnia quae proborum demissorum, non acrium, non pertinacium, non litigiosorum, non acerborum sunt, valde benevolentiam conciliant abalienantque ab iis, in quibus haec non sunt. itaque eadem sunt in adversarios ex contrario conferenda. sed genus hoc totum orationis in iis causis excellet, in quibus minus potest inflammari animus iudicis acri et vehementi quadam incitatione. non enim semper fortis oratio quaeritur, sed saepe placida summissa lenis, quae maxime commendat reos. reos autem appello non eos modo qui arguuntur, sed omnes quorum de re disceptatur; sic enim olim loquebantur. horum igitur exprimere mores oratione iustos, integros, religiosos, timidos, perferentes iniuriarum mirum quiddam valet; et hoc vel in principiis vel in re narranda vel in peroranda tantam habet vim, si est suaviter et cum sensu tractatum, ut saepe plus quam causa valeat. tantum autem efficitur sensu quodam ac ratione dicendi, ut quasi mores oratoris effingat oratio. genere enim quodam sententiarum et genere verborum, adhibita etiam actione leni facilitatemque significanti, efficitur, ut probi, ut bene morati, ut boni viri esse videantur.

Pro Roscio Amerino 75: Qua in re praetereo illud quod mihi maximo argumento ad huius innocentiam poterat esse, in rusticis moribus, in victu arido, in hac horrida incultaque vita istius modi maleficia gigni non solere. Vt non omnem frugem neque arborem in omni agro reperire possis, sic non omne facinus in omni vita nascitur. In urbe luxuries creatur, ex luxurie existat avaritia necesse est, ex avaritia erumpat audacia, inde omnia scelera ac maleficia gignuntur; vita autem haec rustica quam tu agrestem vocas parsimoniae, diligentiae, iustitiae magistra est.

In Catilinam 2.22–25: Postremum autem genus est non solum numero verum etiam genere ipso atque vita quod proprium Catilinae est, de eius dilectu, immo vero de complexu eius ac sinu; quos pexo capillo, nitidos, aut imberbis aut bene barbatos videtis, manicatis et talaribus tunicis, velis amictos, non togis; quorum omnis industria vitae et vigilandi labor in antelucanis cenis expromitur. In his gregibus omnes aleatores, omnes adulteri, omnes impuri impudicique versantur. Hi pueri tam lepidi ac delicati non solum amare et amari neque saltare et cantare sed etiam sicas vibrare et spargere venena didicerunt. Qui nisi exeunt, nisi pereunt, etiam si Catilina perierit, scitote hoc in re publica seminarium Catilinarum futurum. Verum tamen quid sibi isti miseri volunt? num suas secum mulierculas sunt in castra ducturi? Quem ad modum autem illis carere poterunt, his praesertim iam noctibus? Quo autem pacto illi Appenninum atque illas pruinas ac nivis perferent? nisi idcirco se facilius hiemem toleraturos putant, quod nudi in conviviis saltare didicerunt.

O bellum magno opere pertimescendum, cum hanc sit habiturus Catilina scortorum cohortem praetoriam! Instruite nunc, Quirites, contra has tam praeclaras Catilinae copias vestra praesidia vestrosque exercitus. Et primum gladiatori illi confecto et saucio consules imperatoresque vestros opponite; deinde contra illam naufragorum eiectam ac debilitatam manum florem totius Italiae ac robur educite. . . . Neque ego ceteras copias, ornamenta, praesidia vestra cum illius latronis inopia atque egestate conferre debeo. Sed si, omissis his rebus quibus nos suppeditamur, eget ille, senatu, equitibus Romanis, urbe, aerario, vectigalibus, cuncta Italia, provinciis omnibus, exteris nationibus, si his rebus omissis causas ipsas quae inter se confligunt contendere velimus, ex eo ipso quam valde illi iaceant intellegere possumus. Ex hac enim parte pudor pugnat, illinc petulantia; hinc pudicitia, illinc stuprum; hinc fides, illinc fraudatio; hinc pietas, illinc scelus; hinc constantia, illinc furor; hinc

honestas, illinc turpitudo; hinc continentia, illinc libido; hinc denique aequitas, temperantia,
fortitudo, prudentia, virtutes omnes certant cum
iniquitate, luxuria, ignavia, temeritate, cum vitiis
omnibus; postremo copia cum egestate, bona
ratio cum perdita, mens sana cum amentia, bona
denique spes cum omnium rerum desperatione
confligit. In eius modi certamine ac proelio
nonne, si hominum studia deficiant, di ipsi im-
mortales cogant ab his praeclarissimis virtutibus
tot et tanta vitia superari?

PATHOS (ARGUMENT BASED ON EMOTIONAL APPEAL)

De oratore 2.185–87: huic autem est illa dispar
adiuncta ratio orationis, quae alio quodam genere
mentis iudicum permovet impellitque, ut aut od-
erint aut diligant, aut invideant aut salvum velint,
aut metuant aut sperent aut cupiant aut abhor-
reant, aut laetentur aut maereant aut misereantur
aut punire velint aut ad eos motus deducantur,
si qui finitimi sunt et propinqui his ac talibus
animi permotionibus. atque illud optandum est
oratori, ut aliquam permotionem animorum
sua sponte ipsi adferant ad causam iudices ad id,
quod utilitas oratoris feret, accommodatam. facilius est enim currentem, ut aiunt, incitare quam

commovere languentem. sin id aut non erit aut
erit obscurius, sicut medico diligenti, priusquam
conetur aegro adhibere medicinam, non solum
morbus eius cui mederi volet, sed etiam consuetudo valentis et natura corporis cognoscenda
est, sic equidem cum adgredior in ancipiti causa
et gravi ad animos iudicum pertractandos, omni
mente in ea cogitatione curaque versor, ut odorer
quam sagacissime possim quid sentiant, quid ex-
istiment, quid exspectent, quid velint, quo de-
duci oratione facillime posse videantur. si se dant
et, ut ante dixi, sua sponte, quo impellimus, in-
clinant atque propendent, accipio quod datur et
ad id, unde aliquis flatus ostenditur, vela do. sin
est integer quietusque iudex, plus est operis; sunt
enim omnia dicendo excitanda, nihil adiuvante
natura. sed tantam vim habet illa, quae recte a
bono poeta dicta est "flexanima atque omnium
regina rerum oratio," ut non modo inclinantem
excipere aut stantem inclinare, sed etiam adver-
santem ac repugnantem, ut imperator ac fortis
bonus capere possit.

De oratore 2.194–96: quare nolite existimare
me ipsum, . . . cum mihi M.' Aquilius in civitate
retinendus esset, quae in illa causa peroranda

fecerim, sine magno dolore fecisse. quem enim
ego consulem fuisse, imperatorem, ornatum a senatu, ovantem in Capitolium ascendisse meminis-
sem, hunc cum adflictum, debilitatum, maerentem,
in summum discrimen adductum viderem, non
prius sum conatus misericordiam aliis commovere quam misericordia sum ipse captus. sensi
equidem tum magno opere moveri iudices, cum
excitavi maestum ac sordidatum senem et cum
ista feci, quae tu, Crasse, laudas, non arte de qua
quid loquar nescio sed motu magno animi ac dolore, ut discinderem tunicam, ut cicatrices osten-
derem. cum C. Marius maerorem orationis meae
praesens ac sedens multum lacrimis suis adiuvaret
cumque ego illum crebro appellans collegam ei
suum commendarem atque ipsum advocatum ad
communem imperatorum fortunam defendendam
invocarem, non fuit haec sine meis lacrimis, non
sine dolore magno miseratio omniumque deorum
et hominum et civium et sociorum imploratio.
quibus omnibus verbis, quae a me tum sunt habita, si dolor afuisset meus, non modo non misera-
bilis, sed etiam inridenda fuisset oratio mea.

Pro Plancio 101–4: O excubias tuas, Cn. Planci,
miseras, o flebiles vigilias, o noctes acerbas, o

custodiam etiam mei capitis infelicem! si quidem
ego tibi vivus non prosum, qui fortasse mortuus profuissem. Memini enim, memini, neque
umquam obliviscar noctis illius cum tibi vigi-
lanti, adsidenti, maerenti vana quaedam miser
atque inania falsa spe inductus pollicebar, me,
si essem in patriam restitutus, praesentem tibi
gratias relaturum; sin aut vitam mihi fors ad-
emisset aut vis aliqua maior reditum peremis-
set, hos, hos—quos enim ego tum alios animo
intuebar?—omnia tibi illorum laborum praemia
pro me persoluturos. Quid me aspectas, quid
mea promissa repetis, quid meam fidem implo-
ras? Nihil tibi ego tum de meis opibus pollicebar,
sed de horum erga me benevolentia promittebam;
hos pro me lugere, hos gemere, hos decertare pro
meo capite vel vitae periculo velle videbam;
de horum desiderio, luctu, querelis cotidie aliquid tecum simul audiebam; nunc timeo ne nihil
tibi praeter lacrimas queam reddere, quas tu
in meis acerbitatibus plurimas effudisti. Quid
enim possum aliud, nisi maerere, nisi flere, nisi
te cum salute mea complecti? Salutem tibi idem
dare possunt, qui mihi reddiderunt. Te tamen—
exsurge, quaeso!—retinebo et complectar, nec
me solum deprecatorem fortunarum tuarum sed

comitem sociumque profitebor: atque, ut spero, nemo erit tam crudeli animo tamque inhumano nec tam immemor non dicam meorum in bonos meritorum, sed bonorum in me, qui a me mei servatorem capitis divellat ac distrahat. Non ego meis ornatum beneficiis a vobis deprecor, iudices, sed custodem salutis meae, non opibus contendo, non auctoritate, non gratia, sed precibus, sed lacrimis, sed misericordia, mecumque vos simul hic miserrimus et optimus obtestatur parens, et pro uno filio duo patres deprecamur. Nolite, iudices, per vos, per fortunas, per liberos vestros inimicis meis, eis praesertim quos ego pro vestra salute suscepi, dare laetitiam gloriantibus vos iam oblitos mei salutis eius a quo mea salus conservata est hostes exstitisse; nolite animum meum debilitare cum luctu tum etiam metu commutatae vestrae voluntatis erga me; sinite me, quod vobis fretus huic saepe promisi, id a vobis ei persolvere. Teque, C. Flave, oro et obtestor, qui meorum consiliorum in consulatu socius, periculorum particeps, rerum quas gessi adiutor fuisti, meque non modo salvum semper sed etiam ornatum florentemque esse voluisti, ut mihi per hos conserves eum per quem me tibi et his conservatum vides. Plura ne dicam tuae me

etiam lacrimae impediunt vestraeque, iudices,
non solum meae, quibus ego magno in metu
meo subito inducor in spem, vos eosdem in hoc
conservando futuros qui fueritis in me, quoniam
istis vestris lacrimis de illis recordor quas pro me
saepe et multum profudistis.

Arrangement

De oratore 2.307–12: Itaque nunc illuc redeo,
Catule, in quo tu me paulo ante laudabas, ad
ordinem conlocationemque rerum ac locorum.
cuius ratio est duplex: altera, quam affert natura causarum; altera, quae oratorum iudicio et
prudentia comparatur. nam ut aliquid ante rem
dicamus, deinde ut rem exponamus, post ut eam
probemus nostris praesidiis confirmandis, contrariis refutandis, deinde ut concludamus atque
ita peroremus, hoc dicendi natura ipsa praescribit.
ut vero statuamus ea, quae probandi et docendi
causa dicenda sunt, quem ad modum compon-
amus, id est vel maxime proprium oratoris prudentiae. multa enim occurrunt argumenta, multa
quae in dicendo profutura videantur; sed eorum
partim ita levia sunt, ut contemnenda sint; partim, etiam si quid habent adiumenti, sunt nonnumquam eiusmodi, ut insit in iis aliquid vitii

neque tanti sit illud, quod prodesse videatur, ut
cum aliquo malo coniungatur. quae autem utilia
sunt atque firma, si ea tamen, ut saepe fit, valde
multa sunt, ea, quae ex iis aut levissima sunt
aut aliis gravioribus consimilia, secerni arbitror
oportere atque ex oratione removeri. equidem
cum colligo argumenta causarum, non tam ea
numerare soleo quam expendere. et quoniam,
quod saepe iam dixi, tribus rebus homines ad
nostram sententiam perducimus, aut docendo
aut conciliando aut permovendo, una ex tribus
his rebus res prae nobis est ferenda, ut nihil aliud
nisi docere velle videamur; reliquae duae, sicuti
sanguis in corporibus, sic illae in perpetuis ora-
tionibus fusae esse debebunt. nam et principia
et ceterae partes orationis, de quibus paulo post
pauca dicemus, habere hanc vim magno opere
debent, ut ad eorum mentes, apud quos agetur,
[movendas] permanare possint. sed his partibus
orationis, quae, etsi nihil docent argumentando,
persuadendo tamen et commovendo profici-
unt plurimum, quamquam maxime proprius est
locus et in exordiendo et in perorando, degredi
tamen ab eo quod proposueris atque agas, per-
movendorum animorum causa saepe utile est.
itaque vel re narrata et exposita saepe datur ad

commovendos animos degrediendi locus, vel argumentis nostris confirmatis vel contrariis refutatis vel utroque loco, vel omnibus, si habet eam causa dignitatem atque copiam, recte id fieri potest; eaeque causae sunt ad augendum et ad ornandum gravissimae atque plenissimae, quae plurimos exitus dant ad eius modi digressionem, ut iis locis uti liceat, quibus animorum impetus eorum, qui audiunt, aut impellantur aut reflectantur.

Introduction or Prologue
(*Latin* Exordium)

Pro P. Quinctio 1–8, 10: Quae res in civitate duae plurimum possunt, eae contra nos ambae faciunt in hoc tempore, summa gratia et eloquentia; quarum alteram, C. Aquili, vereor, alteram metuo. Eloquentia Q. Hortensi ne me in dicendo impediat, non nihil commoveor, gratia Sex. Naevi ne P. Quinctio noceat, id vero non mediocriter pertimesco. Neque hoc tanto opere querendum videretur, haec summa in illis esse, si in nobis essent saltem mediocria; verum ita se res habet, ut ego, qui neque usu satis et ingenio parum possum, cum patrono disertissimo comparer, P. Quinctius, cui tenues opes, nullae facultates, exiguae

amicorum copiae sunt, cum adversario gratiosis-
simo contendat. Illud quoque nobis accedit in-
commodum, quod M. Iunius, qui hanc causam,
aliquotiens apud te egit, homo et in aliis causis
exercitatus et in hac multum et saepe versatus,
hoc tempore abest nova legatione impeditus, et
ad me ventum est qui, ut summa haberem cet-
era, temporis quidem certe vix satis habui ut rem
tantam, tot controversiis implicatam, possem
cognoscere. Ita quod mihi consuevit in ceteris
causis esse adiumento, id quoque in hac causa
deficit. Nam, quod minus ingenio possum, sub-
sidium mihi diligentia comparavi; quae quanta
sit, nisi tempus et spatium datum sit, intellegi
non potest. Quae quo plura sunt, C. Aquili, eo
te et hos qui tibi in consilio sunt meliore mente
nostra verba audire oportebit, ut multis incom-
modis veritas debilitata tandem aequitate talium
virorum recreetur. Quod si tu iudex nullo prae-
sidio fuisse videbere contra vim et gratiam sol-
itudini atque inopiae, si apud hoc consilium ex
opibus, non ex veritate causa pendetur, profecto
nihil est iam sanctum atque sincerum in civitate,
nihil est quod humilitatem cuiusquam gravitas et
virtus iudicis consoletur. Certe aut apud te et hos
qui tibi adsunt veritas valebit, aut ex hoc loco

repulsa vi et gratia locum ubi consistat reperire non poterit.

Non eo dico, C. Aquili, quo mihi veniat in dubium tua fides et constantia, aut quo non in his quos tibi advocavisti viris lectissimis civitatis spem summam habere P. Quinctius debeat. Quid ergo est? Primum magnitudo periculi summo timore hominem adficit, quod uno iudicio de fortunis omnibus decernit, idque dum cogitat, non minus saepe ei venit in mentem potestatis quam aequitatis tuae, propterea quod omnes quorum in alterius manu vita posita est saepius illud cogitant, quid possit is cuius in dicione ac potestate sunt, quam quid debeat facere. Deinde habet adversarium P. Quinctius verbo Sex. Naevium, re vera huiusce aetatis homines disertissimos, fortissimos, florentissimos nostrae civitatis, qui communi studio summis opibus Sex. Naevium defendunt, si id est defendere, cupiditati alterius obtemperare quo is facilius quem velit iniquo iudicio opprimere possit. Nam quid hoc iniquius aut indignius, C. Aquili, dici aut commemorari potest, quam me qui caput alterius, famam fortunasque defendam priore loco causam dicere? cum praesertim Q. Hortensius qui in hoc iudicio partes accusatoris obtinet contra me sit dicturus,

cui summam copiam facultatemque dicendi natura largita est. Ita fit ut ego qui tela depellere et
volneribus mederi debeam tum id facere cogar
cum etiam telum adversarius nullum iecerit,
illis autem id tempus impugnandi detur cum et
vitandi illorum impetus potestas adempta nobis
erit et, si qua in re, id quod parati sunt facere,
falsum crimen quasi venenatum aliquod telum
iecerint, medicinae faciendae locus non erit. . . .

Cum tot tantisque difficultatibus adfectus
atque adflictus in tuam, C. Aquili, fidem, veritatem, misericordiam P. Quinctius confugerit,
cum adhuc ei propter vim adversariorum non
ius par, non agendi potestas eadem, non magistratus aequus reperiri potuerit, cum ei summam
per iniuriam omnia inimica atque infesta fuerint,
te, C. Aquili, vosque qui in consilio adestis, orat
atque obsecrat ut multis iniuriis iactatam atque
agitatam aequitatem in hoc tandem loco consist-
ere et confirmari patiamini.

Narration or Statement of Facts
(*Latin* Narratio)

Pro Milone 23–29: Quod quo facilius argumentis
perspicere possitis, rem gestam vobis dum breviter
expono, quaeso, diligenter attendite. P. Clodius,

cum statuisset omni scelere in praetura vexare rem
publicam videretque ita tracta esse comitia anno
superiore ut non multos mensis praeturam gerere posset, qui non honoris gradum spectaret, ut
ceteri, sed et L. Paulum conlegam effugere vellet, singulari virtute civem, et annum integrum
ad dilacerandam rem publicam quaereret, subito
reliquit annum suum seseque in annum proxi-
mum transtulit, non, ut fit, religione aliqua, sed
ut haberet, quod ipse dicebat, ad praeturam ger-
endam, hoc est, ad evertendam rem publicam,
plenum annum atque integrum. Occurrebat ei
mancam ac debilem praeturam futuram suam
consule Milone; eum porro summo consensu populi Romani consulem fieri videbat. Contulit se ad
eius competitores, sed ita totam ut petitionem ipse
solus etiam invitis illis gubernaret, tota ut comitia
suis, ut dictitabat, umeris sustineret. Convocabat
tribus, se interponebat, Collinam novam dilectu
perditissimorum civium conscribebat. Quanto
ille plura miscebat, tanto hic magis in dies con-
valescebat. Vbi vidit homo ad omne facinus
paratissimus fortissimum virum, inimicissimum
suum, certissimum consulem, idque intellexit
non solum sermonibus, sed etiam suffragiis populi Romani saepe esse declaratum, palam agere

coepit et aperte dicere occidendum Milonem. Servos agrestis et barbaros, quibus silvas publicas depopulatus erat Etruriamque vexarat, ex Appennino deduxerat, quos videbatis. Res erat minime obscura. Etenim dictitabat palam consulatum Miloni eripi non posse, vitam posse. Significavit hoc saepe in senatu, dixit in contione; quin etiam M. Favonio, fortissimo viro, quaerenti ex eo qua spe fureret Milone vivo, respondit triduo illum aut summum quadriduo esse periturum; quam vocem eius ad hunc M. Catonem statim Favonius detulit. Interim cum sciret Clodius—neque enim erat difficile scire a Lanuvinis—iter sollemne, legitimum, necessarium ante diem XIII Kalendas Februarias Miloni esse Lanuvium ad flaminem prodendum, quod erat dictator Lanuvi Milo, Roma subito ipse profectus pridie est ut ante suum fundum, quod re intellectum est, Miloni insidias conlocaret; atque ita profectus est ut contionem turbulentam in qua eius furor desideratus est, quae illo ipso die habita est, relinqueret, quam, nisi obire facinoris locum tempusque voluisset, numquam reliquisset. Milo autem cum in senatu fuisset eo die quoad senatus est dimissus, domum venit, calceos et vestimenta mutavit, paulisper, dum se uxor, ut fit, comparat, commoratus est, dein profectus id temporis cum iam Clodius, si quidem eo die Romam venturus erat, redire potuisset. Obviam fit ei Clodius, expeditus, in equo, nulla raeda, nullis impedimentis, nullis Graecis comitibus, ut solebat, sine uxore, quod numquam fere: cum hic insidiator, qui iter illud ad caedem faciendam apparasset, cum uxore veheretur in raeda, paenulatus, magno et impedito et muliebri ac delicato ancillarum puerorumque comitatu. Fit obviam Clodio ante fundum eius hora fere undecima aut non multo secus. Statim complures cum telis in hunc faciunt de loco superiore impetum; adversi raedarium occident. Cum autem hic de raeda reiecta paenula desiluisset seque acri animo defenderet, illi qui erant cum Clodio gladiis eductis, partim recurrere ad raedam ut a tergo Milonem adorirentur, partim, quod hunc iam interfectum putarent, caedere incipiunt eius servos qui post erant; ex quibus qui animo fideli in dominum et praesenti fuerunt, partim occisi sunt, partim, cum ad raedam pugnari viderent, domino succurrere prohiberentur, Milonem occisum et ex ipso Clodio audirent et re vera putarent, fecerunt id servi Milonis—dicam enim aperte non derivandi criminis causa, sed ut factum est—nec imperante nec sciente nec praesente domino, quod suos quisque servos in tali re facere voluisset.

Confirmation or Proof
(*Latin* Confirmatio)

De Inventione 1.34, 37, 44, 46: Confirmatio est per quam argumentando nostrae causae fidem et auctoritatem et firmamentum adiungit oratio. . . . Omnes res argumentando confirmantur aut ex eo quod personis aut ex eo quod negotiis est attributum. Ac personis has res attributas putamus: nomen, naturam, victum, fortunam, habitum, affectionem, studia, consilia, facta, casus, orationes. . . . Negotiis autem quae sunt attributa, partim sunt continentia cum ipso negotio, partim in gestione negoti considerantur, partim adiuncta negotio sunt, partim gestum negotium consequuntur. . . . Omnis autem argumentatio quae ex eis locis quos commemoravimus sumetur, aut probabilis aut necessaria debebit esse. Etenim, ut breviter describamus, argumentatio videtur esse inventum aliquo ex genere rem aliquam aut probabiliter ostendens aut necessarie demonstrans. Necessarie demonstrantur ea quae aliter ac dicuntur nec fieri nec probari possunt. . . . Probabile autem est id quod fere solet fieri aut quod in opinione positum est aut quod habet in se ad haec quandam similitudinem, sive id falsum est sive verum.

Pro Milone 52–55: Video adhuc constare, iudices, omnia: Miloni etiam utile fuisse Clodium vivere, illi ad ea quae concupierat optatissimum interitum Milonis; odium fuisse illius in hunc acerbissimum, nullum huius in illum; consuetudinem illius perpetuam in vi inferenda, huius tantum in repellenda; mortem ab illo Miloni denuntiatam et praedicatam palam, nihil umquam auditum ex Milone; profectionis huius diem illi notum, reditus illius huic ignotum fuisse; huius iter necessarium, illius etiam potius alienum; hunc prae se tulisse illo die Roma exiturum, illum eo die se dissimulasse rediturum; hunc nullius rei mutasse consilium, illum causam mutandi consili finxisse; huic, si insidiaretur, noctem prope urbem exspectandam, illi, etiam si hunc non timeret, tamen accessum ad urbem nocturnum fuisse metuendum.

Videamus nunc id quod caput est, locus ad insidias ille ipse ubi congressi sunt utri tandem fuerit aptior. Id vero, iudices, etiam dubitandum et diutius cogitandum est? Ante fundum Clodi quo in fundo propter insanas illas substructiones

facile hominum mille versabantur valentium,
edito adversarii atque excelso loco superiorem
se fore putabat Milo, et ob eam rem eum locum
ad pugnam potissimum elegerat, an in eo loco
est potius exspectatus ab eo, qui ipsius loci spe
facere impetum cogitarat? Res loquitur ipsa,
iudices, quae semper valet plurimum. Si haec
non gesta audiretis, sed picta videretis, tamen
appareret uter esset insidiator, uter nihil mali cog-
itaret, cum alter veheretur in raeda paenulatus,
una sederet uxor. Quid horum non impeditis-
simum? vestitus an vehiculum an comes? quid
minus promptum ad pugnam, cum paenula in-
retitus, raeda impeditus, uxore paene constrictus
esset?—Videte nunc illum, primum egredientem
e villa, subito: cur? vesperi: quid necesse est?
tarde: qui convenit, praesertim id temporis? 'De-
vertit in villam Pompei.' Pompeium ut videret?
sciebat in Alsiensi esse; villam ut perspiceret?
miliens in ea fuerat. Quid ergo erat? morae et
tergiversatio: dum hic veniret, locum relinquere
noluit. Age nunc iter expediti latronis cum Milonis impedimentis comparate. Semper ille antea
cum uxore, tum sine ea; numquam nisi in raeda,
tum in equo; comites Graeculi, quocumque ibat,
etiam cum in castra Etrusca properabat, tum

nugarum in comitatu nihil. Milo qui numquam, tum casu pueros symphoniacos uxoris ducebat et ancillarum greges; ille qui semper secum scorta, semper exoletos, semper lupas duceret, tum neminem, nisi ut virum a viro lectum esse diceres. Cur igitur victus est? Quia non semper viator a latrone, non numquam etiam latro a viatore occiditur; quia, quamquam paratus in imparatos Clodius, ipse Clodius tamen mulier inciderat in viros.

Refutation (Latin Refutatio)

De oratore 2.331: tum suggerenda sunt firmamenta causae coniuncte et infirmandis contrariis et tuis confirmandis. namque una in causis ratio quaedam est eius orationis, quae ad probandam argumentationem valet. ea autem et confirmationem et reprehensionem quaerit; sed quia neque reprehendi quae contra dicuntur possunt, nisi tua confirmes, neque haec confirmari, nisi illa reprehendas, idcirco haec et natura et utilitate et tractatione coniuncta sunt.

De inventione 1.79: Omnis argumentatio reprehenditur, si aut ex eis quae sumpta sunt non conceditur aliquid unum plurave aut his concessis complexio ex his confici negatur, aut si genus ipsum argumentationis vitiosum ostenditur, aut si contra firmam argumentationem alia aeque firma aut firmior ponitur.

Pro Archia 8–11: Si nihil aliud nisi de civitate ac lege dicimus, nihil dico amplius; causa dicta est. Quid enim horum infirmari, Gratti, potest? Heracliaene esse tum ascriptum negabis? Adest vir summa auctoritate et religione et fide, M. Lucullus; qui se non opinari sed scire, non audisse sed vidisse, non interfuisse sed egisse dicit. Adsunt Heraclienses legati, nobilissimi homines, huius iudici causa cum mandatis et cum publico testimonio venerunt; qui hunc ascriptum Heracliae dicunt. Hic tu tabulas desideras Heracliensium publicas, quas Italico bello incenso tabulario interisse scimus omnes? Est ridiculum ad ea quae habemus nihil dicere, quaerere quae habere non possumus, et de hominum memoria tacere, litterarum memoriam flagitare et, cum habeas amplissimi viri religionem, integerrimi municipi ius iurandum fidemque, ea quae depravari nullo modo possunt repudiare, tabulas quas idem dicis solere corrumpi desiderare. An domicilium Romae non habuit is qui tot annis ante civitatem datam

sedem omnium rerum ac fortunarum suarum
Romae conlocavit? An non est professus? Immo
vero eis tabulis professus quae solae ex illa pro-
fessione conlegioque praetorum obtinent publi-
carum tabularum auctoritatem. Nam, cum Appi
tabulae negligentius adservatae dicerentur, Ga-
bini, quam diu incolumis fuit, levitas, post dam-
nationem calamitas omnem tabularum fidem
resignasset, Metellus, homo sanctissimus mod-
estissimusque omnium, tanta diligentia fuit ut ad
L. Lentulum praetorem et ad iudices venerit et
unius nominis litura se commotum esse dixerit.
His igitur in tabulis nullam lituram in nomine
A. Licini videtis. . . . Census nostros requiris.
Scilicet; est enim obscurum proximis censoribus
hunc cum clarissimo imperatore L. Lucullo apud
exercitum fuisse, superioribus cum eodem quae-
store fuisse in Asia, primis Iulio et Crasso nullam
populi partem esse censam. Sed, quoniam census
non ius civitatis confirmat ac tantum modo in-
dicat eum qui sit census ita se iam tum gessisse,
pro cive, eis temporibus is quem tu criminaris
ne ipsius quidem iudicio in civium Romanorum
iure esse versatum et testamentum saepe fecit
nostris legibus, et adiit hereditates civium Romanorum, et in beneficiis ad aerarium delatus est

a L. Lucullo pro consule. Quaere argumenta, si quae potes; numquam enim hic neque suo neque amicorum iudicio revincetur.

Conclusion or Epilogue
(*Latin* Conclusio *or* Peroratio)

Pro Caelio 70, 77–80: Dicta est a me causa, iudices, et perorata. Iam intellegitis quantum iudicium sustineatis, quanta res sit commissa vobis. De vi quaeritis. Quae lex ad imperium, ad maiestatem, ad statum patriae, ad salutem omnium pertinet, quam legem Q. Catulus armata dissensione civium rei publicae paene extremis temporibus tulit, quaeque lex sedata illa flamma consulatus mei fumantis reliquias coniurationis exstinxit, hac nunc lege Caeli adulescentia non ad rei publicae poenas sed ad mulieris libidines et delicias deposcitur. . . .

Conservate igitur rei publicae, iudices, civem bonarum artium, bonarum partium, bonorum virorum. Promitto hoc vobis et rei publicae spondeo, si modo nos ipsi rei publicae satis fecimus, numquam hunc a nostris rationibus seiunctum fore. Quod cum fretus nostra familiaritate promitto, tum quod durissimis se ipse legibus iam obligavit. Non enim potest qui hominem

consularem, cum ab eo rem publicam violatam
esse diceret, in iudicium vocarit ipse esse in re
publica civis turbulentus; non potest qui am-
bitu ne absolutum quidem patiatur esse absolutum ipse impune umquam esse largitor. Habet
a M. Caelio res publica, iudices, duas accusa-
tiones vel obsides periculi vel pignora voluntatis.
Quare oro obtestorque vos, iudices, ut qua in
civitate paucis his diebus Sex. Cloelius absolu-
tus est, quem vos per biennium aut ministrum
seditionis aut ducem vidistis, hominem sine re,
sine fide, sine spe, sine sede, sine fortunis, ore,
lingua, manu, vita omni inquinatum, qui aedis
sacras, qui censum populi Romani, qui memoriam publicam suis manibus incendit, qui Catuli
monumentum adflixit, meam domum diruit, mei
fratris incendit, qui in Palatio atque in urbis oculis servitia ad caedem et inflammandam urbem
incitavit: in ea civitate ne patiamini illum absolutum muliebri gratia, M. Caelium libidini
muliebri condonatum, ne eadem mulier cum
suo coniuge et fratre et turpissimum latronem
eripuisse et honestissimum adulescentem op-
pressisse videatur. Quod cum huius vobis ad-
ulescentiam proposueritis, constituitote ante oculos etiam huius miseri senectutem qui hoc unico

filio nititur, in huius spe requiescit, huius unius
casum pertimescit; quem vos supplicem vestrae
misericordiae, servum potestatis, abiectum non
tam ad pedes quam ad mores sensusque vestros,
vel recordatione parentum vestrorum vel liber-
orum iucunditate sustentate, ut in alterius dolore
vel pietati vel indulgentiae vestrae serviatis. Nolite, iudices, aut hunc iam natura ipsa occidentem
velle maturius exstingui vulnere vestro quam suo
fato, aut hunc nunc primum florescentem fir-
mata iam stirpe virtutis tamquam turbine aliquo
aut subita tempestate pervertere. Conservate
parenti filium, parentem filio, ne aut senectutem
iam prope desperatam contempsisse aut adules-
centiam plenam spei maximae non modo non al-
uisse vos verum etiam perculisse atque adflixisse
videamini. Quem si nobis, si suis, si rei publicae conservatis, addictum, deditum, obstrictum
vobis ac liberis vestris habebitis omniumque
huius nervorum ac laborum vos potissimum,
iudices, fructus uberes diuturnosque capietis.

Style

De oratore 3.19, 22–24: nam cum omnis ex re atque
verbis constet oratio, neque verba sedem habere
possunt, si rem subtraxeris, neque res lumen, si

verba semoveris . . . una est enim . . . eloquentia,
quascumque in oras disputationis regionesve delata est. nam sive de caeli natura loquitur sive de
terrae sive de divina vi sive de humana sive ex in-
feriore loco sive ex aequo sive ex superiore sive ut
impellat homines sive ut doceat sive ut deterreat
sive ut concitet sive ut reflectat sive ut incendat
sive ut leniat sive ad paucos sive ad multos sive
inter alienos sive cum suis sive secum, rivis est
diducta oratio, non fontibus; et, quocumque in-
greditur, eodem est instructu ornatuque comitata.
sed quoniam oppressi iam sumus opinionibus non
modo vulgi, verum etiam hominum leviter erudi-
torum, qui, quae complecti tota nequeunt, haec
facilius divulsa et quasi discerpta contrectant, et
qui tamquam ab animo corpus, sic a sententiis
verba seiungunt, quorum sine interitu fieri neu-
trum potest, non suscipiam oratione mea plus
quam mihi imponitur; tantum significabo brevi
neque verborum ornatum inveniri posse non
partis expressisque sententiis neque esse ullam
sententiam inlustrem sine luce verborum.

De oratore 3.34–36: quod si in nobis, qui adsumus,
tantae dissimilitudines, tam certae res cuiusque
propriae, et in ea varietate fere melius a deteriore

facultate magis quam genere distinguitur, atque
omne laudatur, quod in suo genere perfectum
est, quid censetis, si omnes, qui ubique sunt aut
fuerunt oratores, amplecti voluerimus? nonne
fore ut, quot oratores, totidem paene reperiantur
genera dicendi? ex qua mea disputatione forsitan
occurrat illud, si paene innumerabiles sint quasi
formae figuraeque dicendi specie dispares genere
laudabiles, non posse ea, quae inter se discrep-
ant, isdem praeceptis atque [in] una institutione
formari. quod non est ita; diligentissimeque hoc
est eis, qui instituunt aliquos atque erudiunt, videndum, quo sua quemque natura maxime ferre
videatur. etenim videmus ex eodem quasi ludo
summorum in suo cuiusque genere artificum et
magistrorum exisse discipulos dissimiles inter se
ac tamen laudandos, cum ad cuiusque naturam
institutio doctoris accommodaretur. cuius est
vel maxime insigne illud exemplum, ut ceteras
artes omittamus, quod dicebat Isocrates doctor singularis se calcaribus in Ephoro, contra
autem in Theopompo frenis uti solere. alterum
enim exsultantem verborum audacia reprime-
bat, alterum cunctantem et quasi verecundan-
tem incitabat. neque eos similes effecit inter se,
sed tantum alteri affinxit, de altero limavit, ut id

conformaret in utroque, quod utriusque natura pateretur.

Virtues of Style

CORRECTNESS AND CLARITY

De oratore 3.37–41, 48–49: quinam igitur dicendi est modus melior . . . quam ut Latine, ut plane, ut ornate, ut ad id, quodcumque agetur, apte congruenterque dicamus? atque eorum quidem, quae duo prima dixi, rationem non arbitror expectari a me puri dilucidique sermonis. neque enim conamur docere eum dicere, qui loqui nesciat; nec sperare, qui Latine non possit, hunc ornate esse dicturum; neque vero, qui non dicat quod intellegamus, hunc posse quod admiremur dicere . . . sed omnis loquendi elegantia, quamquam expolitur scientia litterarum, tamen augetur legendis oratoribus et poetis. sunt enim illi veteres, qui ornare nondum poterant ea, quae dicebant, omnes prope praeclare locuti; quorum sermone adsuefacti qui erunt, ne cupientes quidem poterunt loqui nisi Latine. neque tamen erit utendum verbis iis, quibus iam consuetudo nostra non utitur, nisi quando ornandi causa, parce, quod ostendam; sed usitatis ita poterit uti, lectissimis ut utatur is, qui in veteribus erit scriptis studiose et multum volutatus. atque ut Latine loquamur, non solum videndum est, ut et verba efferamus ea, quae nemo iure reprehendat, et ea sic et casibus et temporibus et genere et numero conservemus, ut ne quid perturbatum ac discrepans aut praeposterum sit, sed etiam lingua et spiritus et vocis sonus est ipse moderandus. nolo exprimi litteras putidius, nolo obscurari neglegentius; nolo verba exiliter exanimata exire, nolo inflata et quasi anhelata gravius . . . praetereamus igitur praecepta Latine loquendi, quae puerilis doctrina tradit et subtilior cognitio ac ratio litterarum alit aut consuetudo sermonis cotidiani ac domestici, libri confirmant et lectio veterum oratorum et poetarum. neque vero in illo altero diutius commoremur, ut disputemus, quibus rebus adsequi possimus, ut ea, quae dicamus, intellegantur: Latine scilicet dicendo, verbis usitatis ac proprie demonstrantibus ea, quae significari ac declarari volemus, sine ambiguo verbo aut sermone, non nimis longa continuatione verborum, non valde productis iis, quae similitudinis causa ex aliis rebus transferuntur, non discerptis sententiis, non praeposteris temporibus, non confusis personis, non perturbato ordine.

DISTINCTION (ORNAMENTATION)

De oratore 3.96–101: Ornatur igitur oratio genere primum et quasi colore quodam et suco suo. nam ut gravis, ut suavis, ut erudita sit, ut liberalis, ut admirabilis, ut polita, ut sensus, ut doloris habeat quantum opus sit, non est singulorum articulorum; in toto spectantur haec corpore. ut porro conspersa sit quasi verborum sententiarumque floribus, id non debet esse fusum aequabiliter per omnem orationem, sed ita distinctum, ut sint quasi in ornatu disposita quaedam insignia et lumina. genus igitur dicendi est eligendum, quod maxime teneat eos, qui audiant, et quod non solum delectet, sed etiam sine satietate delectet; non enim a me iam exspectari puto, ut moneam, ut caveatis, ne exilis, ne inculta sit vestra oratio, ne vulgaris, ne obsolete; aliud quiddam maius et ingenia me hortantur vestra et aetates. difficile enim dictu est, quaenam causa sit cur ea, quae maxime sensus nostros impellunt voluptate et specie prima acerrime commovent, ab iis celerrime fastidio quodam et satietate abalienemur. quanto colorum pulchritudine et varietate floridiora sunt in picturis novis pleraque quam in veteribus! quae tamen, etiam si primo aspectu nos ceperunt, diutius non delectant; cum idem nos in antiquis tabulis illo ipso horrido obsoletoque teneamur. quanto molliores sunt et delicatiores in cantu flexiones et falsae voculae quam certae et severae! quibus tamen non modo austeri, sed, si saepius fiunt, multitudo ipsa reclamat. licet hoc videre in reliquis sensibus; unguentis minus diu nos delectari summa et acerrima suavitate conditis quam his moderatis, et magis laudari quod ceram quam quod crocum olere videatur; in ipso tactu esse modum et mollitudinis et levitatis. quin etiam gustatus, qui est sensus ex omnibus maxime voluptarius quique dulcitudine praeter ceteros sensus commovetur, quam cito id, quod valde dulce est, aspernatur ac respuit! quis potione uti aut cibo dulci diutius potest? cum utroque in genere ea, quae leviter sensum voluptate moveant, facillime fugiant satietatem. sic omnibus in rebus voluptatibus maximis fastidium finitimum est; quo hoc minus in oratione miremur, in qua vel ex poetis vel ex oratoribus possumus iudicare concinnam, distinctam, ornatam, festivam, sine intermissione, sine reprehensione, sine varietate, quamvis claris sit coloribus picta vel poesis vel oratio, non posse in delectatione esse diuturna. atque eo ci-

tius in oratoris aut in poetae cincinnis ac fuco
offenditur, quod sensus in nimia voluptate natura, non mente satiantur; in scriptis et in dictis
non aurium solum sed animi iudicio etiam magis
infucata vitia noscuntur. quare "bene" et "praeclare," quamvis nobis saepe dicatur, "belle" et
"festive" nimium saepe nolo. quamquam illa ipsa
exclamatio: "non potest melius" sit velim crebra;
sed habeat tamen illa in dicendo admiratio ac
summa laus umbram aliquam et recessum, quo
magis id, quod erit illuminatum, extare atque
eminere videatur.

De oratore 3.210–12: quamquam id quidem perspicuum est, non omni causae nec auditori neque
personae neque tempori congruere orationis
unum genus. nam et causae capitis alium quendam
verborum sonum requirunt, alium rerum priva-
tarum atque parvarum; et aliud dicendi genus de-
liberationes, aliud laudationes, aliud iudicia, aliud
sermo, aliud consolatio, aliud obiurgatio, aliud
disputatio, aliud historia desiderat. refert etiam
qui audiant, senatus an populus an iudices, fre-
quentes an pauci an singuli, et quales; ipsique oratores qui sint aetate, honore, auctoritate debent

videri; tempus pacis an belli, festinationis an otii.
itaque hoc loco nihil sane est quod praecipi posse
videatur, nisi ut figuram orationis plenioris et ten-
uioris et item illius mediocris ad id, quod agemus,
accommodatam deligamus. ornamentis isdem uti
fere licebit, alias contentius, alias summissius; omnique in re posse quod deceat facere artis et naturae est, scire quid quandoque deceat prudentiae.

Orator 70–74: Sed est eloquentiae sicut reliqua-
rum rerum fundamentum sapientia. Vt enim in
vita sic in oratione nihil est difficilius quam quid
deceat videre. Πρέπον appellant hoc Graeci,
nos dicamus sane decorum; de quo praeclare et
multa praecipiuntur et res est cognitione dignis-
sima; huius ignoratione non modo in vita sed
saepissime et in poematis et in oratione peccatur.
Est autem quid deceat oratori videndum non in
sententiis solum sed etiam in verbis. Non enim
omnis fortuna, non omnis honos, non omnis
auctoritas, non omnis aetas nec vero locus aut
tempus aut auditor omnis eodem aut verborum
genere tractandus est aut sententiarum semperque in omni parte orationis ut vitae quid deceat
est considerandum; quod et in re de qua agitur
positum est et in personis et eorum qui dicunt

et eorum qui audiunt. Itaque hunc locum longe et late patentem philosophi solent in officiis tractare—non cum de recto ipso disputant, nam id quidem unum est—, grammatici in poetis, eloquentes in omni et genere et parte causarum. Quam enim indecorum est de stillicidiis cum apud unum iudicem dicas, amplissimis verbis et locis uti communibus, de maiestate populi Romani summisse et subtiliter! Hic genere toto, at persona alii peccant aut sua aut iudicum aut etiam adversariorum, nec re solum sed saepe verbo; etsi sine re nulla vis verbi est, tamen eadem res saepe aut probatur aut reicitur alio atque alio elata verbo. In omnibusque rebus videndum est quatenus; etsi enim suus cuique modus est, tamen magis offendit nimium quam parum; in quo Apelles pictores quoque eos peccare dicebat qui non sentirent quid esset satis . . . quod si poeta fugit ut maximum vitium, qui peccat etiam, cum probi orationem adfingit improbo stultove sapientis; si denique pictor ille vidit, cum in immolanda Iphigenia tristis Calchas esset, tristior Ulixes, maereret Menelaus, obvolvendum caput Agamemnonis esse, quoniam summum illum luctum penicillo non posset imitari; si denique histrio quid deceat quaerit, quid faciendum oratori

putemus?—sed cum hoc tantum sit, quid in causis earumque quasi membris faciat orator viderit:
illud quidem perspicuum est, non modo partis
orationis sed etiam causas totas alias alia forma
dicendi esse tractandas.

Types or Characters of Style

Orator 69–70: Erit igitur eloquens—hunc enim
auctore Antonio quaerimus—is qui in foro cau-
sisque civilibus ita dicet, ut probet, ut delectet,
ut flectat. Probare necessitatis est, delectare suavi-
tatis, flectere victoriae: nam id unum ex omnibus
ad obtinendas causas potest plurimum. Sed quot
officia oratoris, tot sunt genera dicendi: subtile in
probando, modicum in delectando, vehemens in
flectendo; in quo uno vis omnis oratoris est. Magni
igitur iudici, summae etiam facultatis esse debebit
moderator ille et quasi temperator huius tripertitae
varietatis; nam et iudicabit quid cuique opus sit et
poterit quocumque modo postulabit causa dicere.

Orator 97–99: Tertius est ille amplus copiosus,
gravis ornatus, in quo profecto vis maxima est.
Hic est enim, cuius ornatum dicendi et copiam
admiratae gentes eloquentiam in civitatibus plurimum valere passae sunt, sed hanc eloquentiam,

quae cursu magno sonituque ferretur, quam sus-
picerent omnes, quam admirarentur, quam se
adsequi posse diffiderent. Huius eloquentiae est
tractare animos, huius omni modo permovere.
Haec modo perfringit, modo inrepit in sensus;
inserit novas opiniones, evellit insitas. Sed multum interest inter hoc dicendi genus et superiora.
Qui in illo subtili et acuto elaboravit ut callide
arguteque diceret nec quicquam altius cogitavit,
hoc uno perfecto magnus orator est, et si non
maximus; minimeque in lubrico versabitur et, si
semel constiterit, numquam cadet. Medius ille
autem, quem modicum et temperatum voco, si
modo suum illud satis instruxerit, non extimes-
cet ancipites dicendi incertosque casus; etiam si
quando minus succedet, ut saepe fit, magnum
tamen periculum non adibit: alte enim cadere
non potest. At vero hic noster, quem principem
ponimus, gravis acer ardens, si ad hoc unum est
natus aut in hoc solo se exercuit aut huic generi
studuit uni nec suam copiam cum illis duobus gen-
eribus temperavit, maxime est contemnendus. Ille
enim summissus, quod acute et veteratorie dicit,
sapiens iam, medius suavis, hic autem copiosissi-
mus, si nihil aliud est, vix satis sanus videri solet.
Qui enim nihil potest tranquille, nihil leniter, nihil

partite definite distincte facete dicere, praesertim cum causae partim totae sint eo modo partim aliqua ex parte tractandae si is non praeparatis auribus inflammare rem coepit, furere apud sanos et quasi inter sobrios bacchari vinulentus videtur.

Rhetorica ad Herennium 4.11–15: In gravi consumetur oratio figura si quae cuiusque rei poterunt ornatissima verba reperiri, sive propria sive extranea, ad unam quamque rem adcommodabuntur, et si graves sententiae quae in amplificatione et commiseratione tractantur eligentur, et si exornationes sententiarum aut verborum quae gravitatem habebunt, de quibus post dicemus, adhibebuntur. In hoc genere figurae erit hoc exemplum:

Nam quis est vestrum, iudices, qui satis idoneam possit in eum poenam excogitare qui prodere hostibus patriam cogitarit? Quod maleficium cum hoc scelere conparari, quod huic maleficio dignum supplicium potest inveniri? In iis qui violassent ingenuum, matremfamilias constuprassent, vulnerassent aliquem aut postremo necassent, maxima supplicia maiores consumpserunt; huic truculentissimo ac nefario facinori singularem poenam non reliquerunt. Atque in aliis maleficiis ad singulos aut ad paucos

ex alieno peccato iniuria pervenit; huius sceleris
qui sunt adfines uno consilio universis civibus
atrocissimas calamitates machinantur. O feros animos! O crudeles cogitationes! O derelictos homines ab humanitate! Quid agere ausi sunt, aut cogi-
tare possunt? Quo pacto hostes, revulsis maiorum
sepulcris, diiectis moenibus, ovantes inruerent in
civitatem; quo modo deum templis spoliatis, op-
timatibus trucidatis, aliis abreptis in servitutem,
matribusfamilias et ingenuis sub hostilem libidi-
nem subiectis, urbs acerbissimo concidat incendio
conflagrata; qui se non putant id quod voluerint ad
exitum perduxisse nisi sanctissimae patriae miser-
andum scelerati viderint cinerem. Nequeo verbis
consequi, iudices, indignitatem rei; sed neglegentius
id fero, quia vos mei non egetis. Vester enim vos animus amantissimus rei publicae facile edocet ut eum
qui fortunas omnium voluerit prodere praecipitem
proturbetis ex ea civitate, quam iste hostium spur-
cissimorum dominatu nefario voluerit obruere.

In mediocri figura versabitur oratio si haec, ut
ante dixi, aliquantum demiserimus neque tamen
ad infimum descenderimus, sic:

Quibuscum bellum gerimus, iudices, videtis—
cum sociis qui pro nobis pugnare et imperium

nostrum nobiscum simul virtute et industria con-
servare soliti sunt. Hi cum se et opes suas et copiam
necessario norunt, tum vero nihilominus propter
propinquitatem et omnium rerum societatem quid
omnibus rebus populus Romanus posset scire et
existimare poterant. Hi cum deliberassent nobiscum bellum gerere, quaeso, quae res erat qua freti
bellum suscipere conarentur, cum multo maximam
partem sociorum in officio manere intellegerent;
cum sibi non multitudinem militum, non idoneos
imperatores, non pecuniam publicam praesto esse
viderent, non denique ullam rem quae res pertinet
ad bellum administrandum? Si cum finitimis de
finibus bellum gererent, si totum certamen in uno
proelio positum putarent, tamen omnibus rebus
instructiores et apparatiores venirent; nedum illi
imperium orbis terrae, cui imperio omnes gentes,
reges, nationes partim vi, partim voluntate consen-
serunt, cum aut armis aut liberalitate a populo Romano superati essent, ad se transferre tantulis viribus
conarentur. Quaeret aliquis: "Quid? Fregellani
non sua sponte conati sunt?" Eo quidem isti minus
facile conarentur, quod illi quemadmodum disces-
sent videbant. Nam rerum inperiti, qui unius cuiusque rei de rebus ante gestis exempla petere non
possunt, ii per inprudentiam facillime deducuntur

in fraudem; at ii qui sciunt quid aliis acciderit facile ex aliorum eventis suis rationibus possunt providere. Nulla igitur re inducti, nulla spe freti arma sustulerunt? Quis hoc credet, tantam amentiam quemquam tenuisse ut imperium populi Romani temptare auderet nullis copiis fretus? Ergo aliquid fuisse necessum est. Quid aliud nisi id quod dico potest esse?

In adtenuato figurae genere, id quod ad infimum et cotidianum sermonem demissum est, hoc erit exemplum:

Nam ut forte hic in balneas venit, coepit, postquam perfusus est, defricari; deinde, ubi visum est ut in alveum descenderet, ecce tibi iste de traverso: "Heus," inquit, "adolescens, pueri tui modo me pulsarunt; satis facias oportet." Hic, qui id aetatis ab ignoto praeter consuetudinem appellatus esset, erubuit. Iste clarius eadem et alia dicere coepit. Hic vix: "Tamen," inquit, "sine me considerare." Tum vero iste clamare voce ista quae perfacile cuivis rubores eicere potest; ita petulans est atque acerba: ne ad solarium quidem, ut mihi videtur, sed pone scaenam et in eiusmodi locis exercitata. Conturbatus est adolescens; nec mirum, cui etiam nunc pedagogi lites ad oriculas versarentur inperito huiusmodi conviciorum. Ubi enim iste vidisset scurram exhausto rubore, qui se putaret nihil habere quod de existimatione perderet, ut omnia sine famae detrimento facere posset?

Igitur genera figurarum ex ipsis exemplis intellegi poterant. Erant enim et adtenuata verborum constructio quaedam et item alia in gravitate, alia posita in mediocritate.

Orator 102: Tota mihi causa pro Caecina de verbis interdicti fuit: res involutas definiendo explicavimus, ius civile laudavimus, verba ambigua distinximus. Fuit ornandus in Manilia lege Pompeius: temperata oratione ornandi copiam persecuti sumus. Ius omne retinendae maiestatis Rabiri causa continebatur: ergo in ea omni genere amplificationis exarsimus.

Pro Caecina 51–54: Quae lex, quod senatus consultum, quod magistratus edictum, quod foedus aut pactio, quod, ut ad privatas res redeam, testamentum, quae iudicia aut stipulationes aut pacti et conventi formula non infirmari ac convelli potest, si ad verba rem deflectere velimus, consilium autem eorum qui scripserunt et rationem et auctoritatem relinquamus? Sermo hercule et familiaris et cotidianus non cohaerebit, si verba inter nos aucupabimur; . . . non occurrit uni cuique vestrum aliud alii in omni genere exemplum quod testimonio sit non ex verbis aptum pendere ius; sed verba servire hominum consiliis et auctoritatibus. Ornate et copiose L. Crassus, homo longe eloquentissimus, paulo ante quam nos in forum venimus, iudicio cvirali hanc sententiam defendit et facile, cum contra eum prudentissimus homo, Q. Mucius, diceret, probavit omnibus M'. Curium, qui heres institutus esset ita: "MORTUO POSTUMO FILIO," cum filius non modo non mortuus, sed ne natus quidem esset, heredem esse oportere. Quid? verbis hoc satis erat cautum? Minime. Quae res igitur valuit? Voluntas, quae si tacitis nobis intelligi posset, verbis omnino non uteremur; quia non potest, verba reperta sunt, non quae impedirent sed quae indicarent voluntatem. Lex usum et auctoritatem fundi iubet esse biennium; at utimur eodem iure in aedibus, quae in lege non appellantur. Si via sit immunita, iubet qua velit agere iumentum; potest hoc ex verbis intelligi, licere, si via sit in Brutiis immunita, agere si velit iumentum per M. Scauri Tusculanum. Actio est in auctorem praesentem his verbis: "QUANDOQUE TE IN

IURE CONSPICIO." Hac actione Appius ille Caecus uti non posset, si ita in iure homines verba consectarentur ut rem cuius causa verba sunt non considerarent. Testamento si recitatus heres esset pupillus Cornelius isque iam annos xx haberet, vobis interpretibus amitteret hereditatem.

Pro Lege Manilia (De Imperio Cn. Pompei) 40–42: Age vero, ceteris in rebus qua ille sit temperantia considerate. Vnde illam tantam celeritatem et tam incredibilem cursum inventum putatis? Non enim illum eximia vis remigum aut ars inaudita quaedam gubernandi aut venti aliqui novi tam celeriter in ultimas terras pertulerunt, sed eae res quae ceteros remorari solent non retardarunt. Non avaritia ab instituto cursu ad praedam aliquam devocavit, non libido ad voluptatem, non amoenitas ad delectationem, non nobilitas urbis ad cognitionem, non denique labor ipse ad quietem; postremo signa et tabulas ceteraque ornamenta Graecorum oppidorum quae ceteri tollenda esse arbitrantur, ea sibi ille ne visenda quidem existimavit. Itaque omnes nunc in eis locis Cn. Pompeium sicut aliquem non ex hac urbe missum, sed de caelo delapsum intuentur; nunc denique incipiunt credere fuisse homines

Romanos hac quondam continentia, quod iam
nationibus exteris incredibile ac falso memoriae
proditum videbatur; nunc imperi vestri splendor illis gentibus lucem adferre coepit; nunc in-
tellegunt non sine causa maiores suos tum cum
ea temperantia magistratus habebamus servire
populo Romano quam imperare aliis maluisse.
Iam vero ita faciles aditus ad eum privatorum,
ita liberae querimoniae de aliorum iniuriis esse
dicuntur, ut is qui dignitate principibus excellit
facilitate infimis par esse videatur. Iam quantum consilio, quantum dicendi gravitate et copia
valeat, in quo ipso inest quaedam dignitas im-
peratoria, vos, Quirites, hoc ipso ex loco saepe
cognostis. Fidem vero eius quantam inter socios
existimari putatis quam hostes omnes omnium
generum sanctissimam iudicarint? Humanitate iam
tanta est, ut difficile dictu sit utrum hostes magis
virtutem eius pugnantes timuerint an mansuetudi-
nem victi dilexerint. Et quisquam dubitabit quin
huic hoc tantum bellum permittendum sit qui ad
omnia nostrae memoriae bella conficienda divino
quodam consilio natus esse videatur?

Pro Rabirio Perduellionis Reo 1–5: Etsi, Quirites, non est meae consuetudinis initio dicendi

rationem reddere qua de causa quemque defendam, propterea quod cum omnibus civibus in eorum periculis semper satis iustam mihi causam necessitudinis esse duxi, tamen in hac defensione capitis, famae fortunarumque omnium C. Rabiri proponenda ratio videtur esse offici mei, propterea quod, quae iustissima mihi causa ad hunc defendendum esse visa est, eadem vobis ad absolvendum debet videri. Nam me cum amicitiae vetustas, cum dignitas hominis, cum ratio humanitatis, cum meae vitae perpetua consuetudo ad C. Rabirium defendendum est adhortata, tum vero, ut id studiosissime facerem, salus rei publicae, consulare officium, consulatus denique ipse mihi una a vobis cum salute rei publicae commendatus coegit. Non enim C. Rabirium culpa delicti, non invidia vitae, Quirites, non denique veteres iustae gravesque inimicitiae civium in discrimen capitis vocaverunt, sed ut illud summum auxilium maiestatis atque imperi quod nobis a maioribus est traditum de re publica tolleretur, ut nihil posthac auctoritas senatus, nihil consulare imperium, nihil consensio bonorum contra pestem ac perniciem civitatis valeret, idcirco in his rebus evertendis unius hominis senectus, infirmitas solitudoque temptata est. Quam ob rem

si est boni consulis, cum cuncta auxilia rei publicae labefactari convellique videat, ferre opem
patriae, succurrere saluti fortunisque communibus, implorare civium fidem, suam salutem
posteriorem salute communi ducere, est etiam
bonorum et fortium civium, quales vos omnibus
rei publicae temporibus exstitistis, intercludere
omnis seditionum vias, munire praesidia rei publicae, summum in consulibus imperium, summum
in senatu consilium putare; ea qui secutus sit, laude
potius et honore quam poena et supplicio dignum
iudicare. Quam ob rem labor in hoc defendendo
praecipue meus est, studium vero conservandi
hominis commune mihi vobiscum esse debebit.

Sic enim existimare debetis, Quirites, post
hominum memoriam rem nullam maiorem,
magis periculosam, magis ab omnibus vobis prov-
idendam neque a tribuno pl. susceptam neque a
consule defensam neque ad populum Romanum
esse delatam. Agitur enim nihil aliud in hac
causa, Quirites, nisi ut nullum sit posthac in re
publica publicum consilium, nulla bonorum
consensio contra improborum furorem et auda-
ciam, nullum extremis rei publicae temporibus
perfugium et praesidium salutis. Quae cum ita
sint, primum, quod in tanta dimicatione capitis,

famae fortunarumque omnium fieri necesse est, ab Iove Optimo Maximo ceterisque dis deabusque immortalibus, quorum ope et auxilio multo magis haec res publica quam ratione hominum et consilio gubernatur, pacem ac veniam peto precorque ab eis ut hodiernum diem et ad huius salutem conservandam et ad rem publicam constituendam inluxisse patiantur. Deinde vos, Quirites, quorum potestas proxime ad deorum immortalium numen accedit, oro atque obsecro, quoniam uno tempore vita C. Rabiri, hominis miserrimi atque innocentissimi, salus rei publicae vestris manibus suffragiisque permittitur, adhibeatis in hominis fortunis misericordiam, in rei publicae salute sapientiam quam soletis.

Memory

De oratore 2.351–360: gratiamque habeo Simonidi illi Cio, quem primum ferunt artem memoriae protulisse. dicunt enim, cum cenaret Crannone in Thessalia Simonides apud Scopam, fortunatum hominem et nobilem, cecinissetque id carmen, quod in eum scripsisset, in quo multa ornandi causa poetarum more in Castorem scripta et Pollucem fuissent, nimis illum sordide Simonidi dixisse se dimidium eius ei, quod pactus esset, pro illo car-

mine daturum; reliquum a suis Tyndaridis, quos
aeque laudasset, peteret, si ei videretur. paulo
post esse ferunt nuntiatum Simonidi, ut prodi-
ret; iuvenes stare ad ianuam duos quosdam, qui
eum magno opere vocarent; surrexisse illum,
prodisse, vidisse neminem. hoc interim spatio
conclave illud, ubi epularetur Scopas, concidisse;
ea ruina ipsum cum cognatis oppressum suis interisse. quos cum humare vellent sui neque possent obtritos internoscere ullo modo, Simonides
dicitur ex eo, quod meminisset quo eorum loco
quisque cubuisset, demonstrator unius cuiusque
sepeliendi fuisse. hac tum re admonitus invenisse
fertur ordinem esse maxime, qui memoriae
lumen afferret. itaque iis, qui hanc partem ingenii exercerent, locos esse capiendos et ea, quae
memoria tenere vellent, effingenda animo atque
in iis locis collocanda: sic fore, ut ordinem rerum
locorum ordo conservaret, res autem ipsas rerum
effigies notaret atque ut locis pro cera, simulacris
pro litteris uteremur. qui sit autem oratori memoriae fructus, quanta utilitas, quanta vis, quid
me attinet dicere? tenere quae didiceris in ac-
cipienda causa, quae ipse cogitaris? omnis fixas
esse in animo sententias? omnem descriptum
verborum apparatum? ita audire vel eum unde

discas vel eum, cui respondendum sit, ut illi non infundere in aures tuas orationem, sed in animo videantur inscribere? itaque soli qui memoria vigent, sciunt, quid et quatenus et quomodo dicturi sint, quid responderint, quid supersit; eidemque multa ex aliis causis aliquando a se acta, multa ab aliis audita meminerunt. quare confiteor equidem huius boni naturam esse principem— sicut earum rerum, de quibus ante locutus sum, omnium; sed haec ars tota dicendi . . . habet hanc vim, non ut totum aliquid, cuius in ingeniis nostris pars nulla sit, pariat et procreet, verum ut ea, quae sunt orta iam in nobis et procreata, educet atque confirmet—,verum tamen neque tam acri memoria fere quisquam est, ut non dispositis notatisque rebus ordinem verborum aut nominum aut sententiarum complectatur, neque vero tam hebeti, ut nihil hac consuetudine et exercitatione adiuvetur. vidit enim hoc prudenter sive Simonides sive alius quis invenit, ea maxime animis effingi nostris, quae essent a sensu tradita atque impressa; acerrimum autem ex omnibus nostris sensibus esse sensum videndi; quare facillime animo teneri posse, si ea, quae perciperentur auribus aut cogitatione, etiam oculorum commendatione animis traderentur; ut res caecas et ab aspectus iudicio remotas conformatio quaedam et imago et figura ita notaret, ut ea, quae cogitando complecti vix possemus, intuendo quasi teneremus. his autem formis atque corporibus, sicut omnibus, quae sub aspectum veniunt, sede opus est; etenim corpus intellegi sine loco non potest. quare, ne in re nota et pervolgata multus et insolens sim, locis est utendum multis, illustribus, explicatis, modicis intervallis, imaginibus autem agentibus, acribus, insignitis, quae occurrere celeriter, quae percutere animum possint. quam facultatem et exercitatio dabit, ex qua consuetudo gignitur . . . sed verborum memoria, quae minus est nobis necessaria, maiore imaginum varietate distinguitur. multa enim sunt verba, quae quasi articuli conectunt membra orationis, quae formari similitudine nulla possunt; eorum fingendae nobis sunt imagines, quibus semper utamur. rerum memoria propria est oratoris; eam singulis personis bene positis notare possumus, ut sententias imaginibus, ordinem locis comprehendamus. neque verum est, quod ab inertibus dicitur opprimi memoriam imaginum pondere et obscurari etiam id, quod per se natura tenere potuisset. vidi enim ego summos homines et divina prope memoria, Athenis Charmadam, in Asia, quem vivere hodie aiunt Scepsium Metrodorum, quorum uterque tamquam litteris in cera, sic se aiebat imaginibus in iis locis, quos haberet, quae meminisse vellet, perscribere. quare hac exercitatione non eruenda memoria est, si est nulla naturalis; sed certe, si latet, evocanda est.

Delivery

Brutus 142: . . . ut verum videretur in hoc illud, quod Demosthenem ferunt ei, qui quaesivisset quid primum esset in dicendo, actionem; quid secundum, idem et idem tertium respondisse. Nulla res magis penetrat in animos eosque fingit format flectit talisque oratores videri facit, qualis ipsi se videri volunt.

De oratore 3.213–27: Sed haec ipsa omnia perinde sunt ut aguntur. actio, inquam, in dicendo una dominatur. sine hac summus orator esse in numero nullo potest, mediocris hac instructus summos saepe superare. huic primas dedisse Demosthenes dicitur, cum rogaretur quid in dicendo esset primum, huic secundas huic tertias. quo mihi melius etiam illud ab Aeschine dictum videri solet; qui cum propter ignominiam iudicii cessisset Athenis et se Rhodum contulisset, rog-

atus a Rhodiis legisse fertur orationem illam
egregiam, quam in Ctesiphontem contra Demosthenem dixerat; qua perlecta petitum est ab eo
postridie, ut legeret illam etiam, quae erat contra
a Demosthene pro Ctesiphonte edita; quam cum
suavissima et maxima voce legisset, admirantibus
omnibus: "quanto," inquit, "magis miraremini,
si audissetis ipsum!" ex quo satis significavit
quantum esset in actione, qui orationem ean-
dem aliam fore putarit actore mutato. quid fuit
in Graccho, quem tu melius, Catule, meministi,
quod me puero tanto opere ferretur? "quo me
miser conferam? quo vertam? in Capitoliumne?
at fratris sanguine redundat. an domum? ma-
tremne ut miseram lamentantemque videam et
abiectam?" quae sic ab illo acta esse constabat
oculis, voce, gestu, inimici ut lacrimas tenere non
possent. haec eo dico pluribus, quod genus hoc
totum oratores, qui sunt veritatis ipsius actores,
reliquerunt, imitatores autem veritatis histriones
occupaverunt. ac sine dubio in omni re vincit
imitationem veritas; sed ea si satis in actione ef-
ficeret ipsa per sese, arte profecto non egeremus.
verum quia animi permotio, quae maxime aut
declaranda aut imitanda est actione, perturbata
saepe ita est ut obscuretur ac paene obruatur,

discutienda sunt ea, quae obscurant, et ea, quae
sunt eminentia et prompta sumenda. omnis enim
motus animi suum quendam a natura habet vol-
tum et sonum et gestum; corpusque totum hominis et eius omnis voltus omnesque voces, ut nervi
in fidibus, ita sonant, ut motu animi quoque sunt
pulsae. nam voces ut chordae sunt intentae, quae
ad quemque tactum respondeant, acuta, gravis,
cita, tarda, magna, parva; quas tamen inter omnis
est suo quaeque in genere mediocris. atque etiam
illa sunt ab his delapsa plura genera leve, asperum,
contractum, diffusum, continenti spiritu, intermisso, fractum, scissum flexo sono extenuatum,
inflatum. nullum est enim horum generum, quod
non arte ac moderatione tractetur. hi sunt actori,
ut pictori, expositi ad variandum colores. aliud
enim vocis genus iracundia sibi sumat, acutum,
incitatum, crebro incidens . . . aliud metus, demissum et haesitans et abiectum . . . aliud vis,
contentum, vehemens, imminens quadam incitatione gravitatis . . . aliud voluptas effusum et
tenerum, hilaratum ac remissum. . . .

Omnis autem hos motus subsequi debet ges-
tus, non hic verba exprimens scaenicus, sed uni-
versam rem et sententiam non demonstratione
sed significatione declarans, laterum inflexione

hac forti ac virili, non ab scaena et histrionibus, sed ab armis aut etiam a palaestra. manus autem minus arguta, digitis subsequens verba, non exprimens; brachium procerius proiectum quasi quoddam telum orationis; supplosio pedis in contentionibus aut incipiendis aut finiendis. sed in ore sunt omnia. in eo autem ipso dominatus est omnis oculorum; quo melius nostri illi senes, qui personatum ne Roscium quidem magno opere laudabant. animi est enim omnis actio et imago animi voltus indices oculi. nam haec est una pars corporis, quae, quot animi motus sunt, tot significationes et commutationes possit efficere. neque vero est quisquam qui eadem conivens efficiat. Theophrastus quidem Tauriscum quendam dicit actorem aversum solitum esse dicere, qui in agendo contuens aliquid pronuntiaret. quare oculorum est magna moderatio. nam oris non est nimium mutanda species, ne aut ad ineptias aut ad pravitatem aliquam deferamur. oculi sunt, quorum tum intentione, tum remissione, tum coniectu, tum hilaritate motus animorum significemus apte cum genere ipso orationis. est enim actio quasi sermo corporis, quo magis menti congruens esse debet. oculos autem natura nobis, ut equo et leoni saetas, caudam, auris, ad motus animorum

declarandos dedit. quare in hac nostra actione
secundum vocem voltus valet: is autem oculis gubernatur. atque in eis omnibus, quae sunt actionis,
inest quaedam vis a natura data. quare etiam hac
imperiti, hac volgus, hac denique barbari maxime commoventur. verba enim neminem movent
nisi eum, qui eiusdem linguae societate coniunc-
tus est, sententiaeque saepe acutae non acutorum
hominum sensus praetervolant; actio, quae prae
se motum animi fert, omnis movet; isdem enim
omnium animi motibus concitantur et eos isdem
notis et in aliis agnoscunt et in se ipsi indicant.

Ad actionis autem usum atque laudem maximam, sine dubio partem vox obtinet; quae primum
est optanda nobis; deinde quaecumque erit, ea tu-
enda. de quo illud iam nihil ad hoc praecipiendi
genus quem admodum voci serviatur; equidem
tamen magno opere censeo serviendum; sed illud
videtur ab huius nostri sermonis officio non abhorrere, quod, ut dixi paulo ante, plurimis in
rebus quod maxime est utile, id nescio quo pacto
etiam decet maxime. nam ad vocem obtinendam
nihil est utilius quam crebra mutatio, nihil perni-
ciosius quam effusa sine intermissione contentio.
quid? ad auris nostras et actionis suavitatem quid
est vicissitudine et varietate et commutatione ap-

tius? itaque idem Gracchus . . . cum eburneola solitus est habere fistula, qui staret occulte post ipsum cum contionaretur, peritum hominem, qui inflaret celeriter eum sonum, quo illum aut remissum excitaret aut a contentione revocaret . . . in omni voce . . . est quiddam medium sed suum cuique voci. hinc gradatim ascendere vocem utile et suave est—nam a principio clamare agreste quiddam est—et idem illud ad firmandam est vocem salutare. deinde est quiddam contentionis extremum, quod tamen interius est quam acutissimus clamor, quo te fistula progredi non sinet, et tamen ab ipsa contentione revocabit. est item contra quiddam in remissione gravissimum quoque tamquam sonorum gradibus descenditur. haec varietas et hic per omnes sonos vocis cursus et se tuebitur et actioni afferet suavitatem. et fistulatorem domi relinquetis, sensum huius consuetudinis vobiscum ad forum deferetis.

The Value of Imitating Good Models of Speaking

De oratore 2.88–92, 96: Atque ut a familiari nostro exordiar, hunc ego, Catule, Sulpicium primum in causa parvola adulescentulum audivi

voce et forma et motu corporis et reliquis rebus
aptis ad hoc munus, de quo quaerimus, oratione
autem celeri et concitata, quod erat ingenii, sed
verbis effervescentibus et paulo nimium redun-
dantibus, quod erat aetatis. non sum aspernatus;
volo enim se efferat in adulescente fecunditas.
nam facilius sicut in vitibus revocantur ea quae
se nimium profuderunt quam, si nihil valet materies, nova sarmenta cultura excitantur; item
volo esse in adulescente unde aliquid amputem.
non enim potest in eo sucus esse diuturnus,
quod nimis celeriter est maturitatem adsecutum.
vidi statim indolem neque dimisi tempus et eum
sum cohortatus ut forum sibi ludum putaret esse
ad discendum, magistrum autem quem vellet el-
igeret; me quidem si audiret, L. Crassum. quod
iste adripuit et ita sese facturum confirmavit atque
etiam addidit, gratiae scilicet causa, me quoque sibi
magistrum futurum. vix annus intercesserat ab
hoc sermone cohortationis meae, cum iste ac-
cusavit C. Norbanum, defendente me. non est
credibile quid interesse mihi sit visum inter eum,
qui tum erat et qui anno ante fuerat. omnino in
illud genus eum Crassi magnificum atque prae-
clarum natura ipsa ducebat, sed ea non satis pro-
ficere potuisset, nisi eodem studio atque imita-

tione intendisset atque ita dicere consuesset, ut
tota mente Crassum atque omni animo intuere-
tur. ergo hoc sit primum in praeceptis meis, ut
demonstremus quem imitetur, [atque ita ut quae
maxime excellant in eo quem imitabitur, ea diligentissime persequatur]. tum accedat exercitatio, qua illum quem delegerit imitando effingat
atque ita exprimat <at non> ita ut multos imitatores saepe cognovi, qui aut ea, quae facilia sunt,
aut etiam illa, quae insignia ac paene vitiosa, con-
sectentur imitando. nihil est facilius quam am-
ictum imitari alicuius aut statum aut motum. si
vero etiam vitiosi aliquid est, id sumere et in eo
vitiosum esse non magnum est, ut ille, qui nunc
etiam amissa voce furit in republica, Fufius nervos
in dicendo C. Fimbriae, quos tamen habuit ille,
non adsequitur, oris pravitatem et verborum lati-
tudinem imitatur. sed tamen ille nec deligere scivit
cuius potissimum similis esset, et in eo ipso quem
delegerat imitari etiam vitia voluit. qui autem ita
faciet ut oportet, primum vigilet necesse est in de-
ligendo; deinde, quem probavit in eo quae maxime excellent, ea diligentissime persequatur. . . .

Hanc igitur similitudinem qui imitatione adsequi volet, cum exercitationibus crebris atque
magnis tum scribendo maxime persequatur. quod

si noster Sulpicius faceret, multo eius oratio esset pressior; in qua nunc interdum, ut in herbis rustici solent dicere in summa ubertate, inest luxuries quaedam, quae stilo depascenda est.

The Value of Writing to Prepare for Effective Speaking

De oratore 1.149–55: Equidem probo ista, Crassus inquit, quae vos facere soletis, ut causa aliqua posita consimili causarum earum quae in forum deferuntur, dicatis quam maxime ad veritatem accommodate. sed plerique in hoc vocem modo, neque eam scienter, et vires exercent suas et linguae celeritatem incitant verborumque frequentia delectantur. in quo fallit eos quod audierunt, dicendo homines ut dicant efficere solere. vere enim etiam illud dicitur, perverse dicere homines perverse dicendo facillime consequi. quam ob rem in istis ipsis exercitationibus etsi utile est etiam subito saepe dicere, tamen illud utilius, sumpto spatio ad cogitandum, paratius atque accuratius dicere. caput autem est quod ut vere dicam minime facimus—est enim magni laboris, quem plerique fugimus—quam plurimum scribere. <stilus est> stilus optimus et praestantissimus dicendi

effector ac magister; neque iniuria: nam si subi-
tam et fortuitam orationem commentatio et cog-
itatio facile vincit, hanc ipsam profecto adsidua
ac diligens scriptura superabit. omnes enim, sive
artis sunt loci sive ingenii cuiusdam atque prudentiae, qui modo insunt in ea re de qua scri-
bimus, inquirentibus nobis omnique acie ingenii
contemplantibus ostendunt se et occurrunt; omnesque sententiae verbaque omnia quae sunt
cuiusque generis <maxime propria> maximeque
inlustria, sub acumen stili subeant et succedant
necesse est; tum ipsa conlocatio conformatioque
verborum perficitur in scribendo, non poetico
sed quodam oratorio numero et modo. haec
sunt quae clamores et admirationes in bonis oratoribus efficiunt, neque ea quisquam, nisi diu
multumque scriptitarit, etiam si vehementissime
se in his subitis dictionibus exercuerit, consequetur. et qui a scribendi consuetudine ad dicendum
venit, hanc adfert facultatem, ut etiam subito si
dicat, tamen illa quae dicantur similia scriptorum
esse videantur; atque etiam, si quando in dicendo
scriptum attulerit aliquid, cum ab eo discesserit,
reliqua similis oratio consequetur. ut concitato
navigio cum remiges inhibuerunt, retinet tamen
ipsa navis motum et cursum suum intermisso

impetu pulsuque remorum, sic in oratione perpetua, cum scripta deficiunt, parem tamen obtinet oratio reliqua cursum scriptorum similitudine et vi concitata. in cotidianis autem
commentationibus equidem mihi adulescentulus
proponere solebam illam exercitationem maxime,
qua C. Carbonem nostrum illum inimicum solitum esse uti sciebam, ut aut versibus propositis
quam maxime gravibus aut oratione aliqua lecta
ad eum finem quem memoria possem compre-
hendere, eam rem ipsam quam legissem verbis
aliis quam maxime possem lectis pronuntiarem.
sed post animadverti hoc esse in hoc vitii, quod ea
verba, quae maxime cuiusque rei propria quaeque
essent ornatissima atque optima occupasset aut
Ennius, si ad eius versus me exercerem, aut Gracchus si eius orationem mihi forte posuissem: ita,
si isdem verbis uterer nihil prodesse, si aliis etiam
obesse, cum minus idoneis uti consuescerem.
postea mihi placuit eoque sum usus adulescens,
ut summorum oratorum Graecas orationes ex-
plicarem. quibus lectis hoc assequebar, ut cum
ea quae legerem Graece, Latine redderem, non
solum optimis verbis uterer et tamen usitatis, sed
etiam exprimerem quaedam verba imitando, quae
nova nostris essent, dum modo essent idonea.

The Requirements and Education of the Ideal Speaker

De oratore 1.6–20: Ac mihi quidem saepenumero in summos homines ac summis ingeniis praeditos intuenti quaerendum esse visum est quid esset cur plures in omnibus artibus quam in dicendo admirabiles extitissent. nam quocumque te animo et cogitatione converteris, permultos excellentis in quoque genere videbis non mediocrium artium sed prope maximarum. quis enim est qui si clarorum hominum scientiam rerum gestarum vel utilitate vel magnitudine metiri velit, non anteponat oratori imperatorem? quis autem dubitet quin belli duces praestantissimos ex hac una civitate paene innumerabiles, in dicendo autem excellentis vix paucos proferre possimus? iam vero, consilio ac sententia qui regere ac gubernare rem p(ublicam) possent multi nostra plures patrum memoria atque etiam maiorum extiterunt, cum boni perdiu nulli, vix autem singulis aetatibus singuli tolerabiles oratores invenirentur. ac ne qui forte cum aliis studiis quae reconditis in artibus atque in quadam varietate litterarum versentur magis hanc dicendi rationem quam cum imperatoris laude aut cum boni senatoris prudentia

comparandam putet, convertat animum ad ea
ipsa artium genera circumspiciatque qui in iis
floruerint quamque multi: sic facillime quanta
oratorum sit et semper fuerit paucitas iudicabit.
neque enim te fugit laudandarum artium omnium procreatricem quandam et quasi parentem
eam quam φιλοσοφίαν Graeci vocant ab hominibus doctissimis iudicari, in qua difficile est
numerare quot viri quanta scientia quantaque
in suis studiis varietate et copia fuerint qui non
una aliqua in re separatim elaborarint, sed omnia
quaecumque essent vel scientiae pervestigatione
vel disserendi ratione comprehenderint. quis ignorat ii qui mathematici vocantur quanta in ob-
scuritate rerum et quam recondita in arte et mul-
tiplici subtilique versentur? quo tamen in genere
ita multi perfecti homines extiterunt, ut nemo
fere studuisse ei scientiae vehementius videatur
quin quod voluerit consecutus sit. quis musi-
cis, quis huic studio litterarum quod profitentur
ei qui grammatici vocantur penitus se dedit quin
omnem illarum artium paene infinitam vim et
materiam scientia et cogitatione comprehen-
derit? vere mihi hoc videor esse dicturus, ex
omnibus iis qui in harum artium liberalissimis
studiis sint doctrinisque versati minimam co-

piam poetarum <et oratorum> egregiorum ex-
titisse. atque in hoc ipso numero in quo perraro
exoritur aliquis excellens, si diligenter et ex nostrorum et ex Graecorum copia comparare voles,
multo tamen pauciores oratores quam poetae
boni reperientur. quod hoc etiam mirabilius debet
videri, quia ceterarum artium studia fere reconditis atque abditis e fontibus hauriuntur, dicendi
autem omnis ratio in medio posita communi
quodam in usu atque in hominum more et sermone versatur, ut in ceteris id maxime excellat
quod longissime sit ab imperitorum intellegentia
sensuque diiunctum, in dicendo autem vitium
vel maximum sit a vulgari genere orationis atque
a consuetudine communis sensus abhorrere. ac
ne illud quidem vere dici potest aut pluris ceteris
artibus inservire aut maiore delectatione aut spe
uberiore aut praemiis ad perdiscendum amplior-
ibus commoveri. atque ut omittam Graeciam quae
semper eloquentiae princeps esse voluit atque
illas omnium doctrinarum inventrices Athenas
in quibus summa dicendi vis et inventa est et per-
fecta, in hac ipsa civitate profecto nulla unquam
vehementius quam eloquentiae studia viguerunt.
nam posteaquam imperio omnium gentium con-
stituto diuturnitas pacis otium confirmavit, nemo

fere laudis cupidus adulescens non sibi ad dicendum studio omni enitendum putavit. ac primo
quidem totius rationis ignari qui neque exercitationis ullam viam neque aliquod praeceptum
artis esse arbitrarentur, tantum quantum ingenio et cogitatione poterant consequebantur. post
autem auditis oratoribus Graecis cognitisque
eorum litteris adhibitisque doctoribus incredibili
quodam nostri homines discendi studio flagrav-
erunt. excitabat eos magnitudo et varietas mul-
titudoque in omni genere causarum, ut ad eam
doctrinam quam suo quisque studio consecutus
esset adiungeretur usus frequens qui omnium
magistrorum praecepta superaret. erant autem
huic studio maxima quae nunc quoque sunt exposita praemia vel ad gratiam vel ad opes vel ad
dignitatem, ingenia vero, ut multis rebus possumus iudicare, nostrorum hominum multum ceteris hominibus omnium gentium praestiterunt.
quibus de causis quis non iure miretur ex omni
memoria aetatum temporum civitatum tam ex-
iguum oratorum numerum inveniri?

Sed nimirum maius est hoc quiddam quam
homines opinantur et pluribus ex artibus stu-
diisque collectum. quid enim quis aliud in maxima discentium multitudine summa magistrorum

copia praestantissimis hominum ingeniis infinita
causarum varietate amplissimis eloquentiae propositis praemiis esse causae putet nisi rei quandam
incredibilem magnitudinem ac difficultatem? est
enim et scientia comprendenda rerum pluri-
marum sine qua verborum volubilitas inanis
atque inridenda est et ipsa oratio conformanda
non solum electione sed etiam constructione verborum et omnes animorum motus quos hominum generi rerum natura tribuit penitus per-
noscendi, quod omnis vis ratioque dicendi in
eorum qui audiunt mentibus aut sedandis aut ex-
citandis expromenda est. accedat eodem oportet
lepos quidam facetiaeque et eruditio libero digna
celeritasque et brevitas et respondendi et laces-
sendi subtili venustate atque urbanitate coniuncta. tenenda praeterea est omnis antiquitas
exemplorumque vis neque legum aut iuris civilis
scientia neglegenda est. nam quid ego de actione
ipsa plura dicam quae motu corporis, quae gestu,
quae vultu, quae vocis conformatione ac varietate moderanda est? quae sola per se ipsa quanta
sit histrionum levis ars et scaena declarat in qua
cum omnes in oris et vocis et motus moderatione
elaborent, quis ignorat quam pauci sint fuer-
intque quos animo aequo spectare possimus?

quid dicam de thesauro rerum omnium memoria? quae nisi custos inventis cogitatisque rebus
et verbis adhibeatur, intellegimus omnia, etiam si
praeclarissima fuerint in oratore, peritura. quam
ob rem mirari desinamus quae causa sit eloquen-
tium paucitatis, cum ex illis rebus universis eloquentia constet quibus in singulis elaborare
permagnum est, hortemurque potius liberos
nostros ceterosque quorum gloria nobis et dignitas cara est, ut animo rei magnitudinem com-
plectantur neque eis aut praeceptis aut magistris
aut exercitationibus quibus utuntur omnes, sed
aliis quibusdam se id quod expetunt consequi
posse confidant. ac mea quidem sententia nemo
poterit esse omni laude cumulatus orator, nisi
erit omnium rerum magnarum atque artium scientiam consecutus. etenim ex rerum cognitione
efflorescat et redundet oportet oratio; quae nisi
subest res ab oratore percepta et cognita, inanem
quamdam habet elocutionem et paene puerilem.

GLOSSARY

ACTIO: See *delivery*.

AEDILE: Roman magistrate, elected annually to serve for one year; aediles were charged with the care of buildings, temples, markets, the public games, and grain supply.

AESCHINES: Athenian orator and politician (ca. 397–ca. 322 BC); opponent of Demosthenes in the famous Ctesiphon trial.

AESCHINES SOCRATICUS: Devoted follower of Socrates, who taught oratory and wrote speeches as well as Socratic dialogues (fourth century BC).

AGAMEMNON: In mythology, the son of Atreus, brother of Menelaus, husband of Clytemnestra; the king of Mycenae and leader of the Greek expedition to Troy.

ALSIUM: One of the oldest towns in Etruria.

ANTONIUS: Marcus Antonius (143–87 BC), one of the great orators of his generation, mentor to Cicero, and a leading character in Cicero's dialogue, *De oratore*; grandfather of the triumvir Mark Antony.

ANTONY, MARK: Marcus Antonius (ca. 82–30 BC), grandson of M. Antonius, the orator; staunch supporter of Julius Caesar; attacked by Cicero in his *Philippics*; joined with Octavian and Lepidus as member of the Second Triumvirate. After joining forces with Cleopatra and suffering defeat at the battle of Actium, he committed suicide.

APELLES: Famous Greek painter from Colophon in Asia Minor. He was the preferred portrait artist of Alexander the Great; his painting of Aphrodite of Cos was considered a masterpiece.

APOLOGY: The speech delivered by Socrates, as related by Plato, in defense of the charge of impiety leveled against him in 399 BC.

APPIAN WAY: The *Via Appia*, the first great Roman road, built in 312 BC, running from Rome to Capua.

APPIUS CLAUDIUS CAECUS: Famous Roman senator and censor (312–308 BC), who was responsible for building the Appian Way and the first aqueduct to bring water to Rome. In 280 BC, old and by then blind, he spoke vigorously in the Senate against making peace with the enemy general Pyrrhus.

APPROPRIATENESS: One of the four, traditional "virtues," or qualities of style.

AQUILIUS: Gaius Aquilius, chief assessor in the trial of Quinctius, 81 BC.

AQUILLIUS: Manius Aquillius, consul in 101 BC; prosecuted for embezzlement in 97, but successfully defended by Marcus Antonius.

ARCHIAS: Greek poet, teacher and friend of Cicero, who defended him in a trial concerning citizenship in 62 BC.

ARISTOTLE: Greek philosopher (384–322 BC), student of Plato, tutor of Alexander the Great, and founder of the philosophical school known as the Peripatos; author of *On Rhetoric*, as well as many other important works on philosophy and natural science.

ARRANGEMENT: The second of the standard "activities of the orator," consisting of ordering the material of a speech.

ARTISTIC PROOF: Proof that a speaker creates by employing his own art, including sources of persuasion based in *logos*, *ethos*, and *pathos*.

ASIA: In antiquity, the named applied especially to what is now called Asia Minor, the geographical region corresponding roughly to modern Turkey. Most of it became the Roman province of Asia in 133 BC.

ASPASIA: The mistress of Athenian general Pericles, reputed to have taught rhetoric and to have participated in dialogues with Socrates and other influential thinkers.

BRUTTIUM: The southern region of Italy, originally inhabited by the Bruttii.

BRUTUS: Rhetorical treatise written by Cicero in 46 BC, dedicated to Marcus Junius Brutus (later one of Caesar's assassins); dedicated largely to presenting a history of Roman oratory.

CAECINA: Aulus Caecina, represented by Cicero in a complicated case involving the inheritance of land.

CAELIUS: Marcus Caelius Rufus (88 or 87–48 BC), protégé and later correspondent of Cicero, defended by him on a charge of violence in 56 BC.

CAESAR: Gaius Julius Caesar (102–44 BC), famous general, member of the so-called First Triumvirate, later dictator of Rome, assassinated on the Ides (15th) of March, 44 BC.

CALCHAS: A seer who accompanied the Greek fleet to Troy.

CARBO: Gaius Papirius Carbo, consul in 120 BC and one of the finest orators of his generation. He was prosecuted by the young Crassus in 119 and committed suicide, fearing that the death penalty would be imposed.

CASTOR: In mythology, one of the so-called Dioscuri, twin sons of Zeus and Leda; brother of Pollux.

CATILINE: Lucius Sergius Catilina, an impoverished senator who engineered an attempted coup against the state in 63 BC, during Cicero's consulship. Cicero delivered four famous speeches against him (*In Catilinam*), and thwarted the attempt. He was killed with an army of supporters in 62.

CATO: Marcus Porcius Cato the Younger (95–46 BC), chief antagonist of Caesar and the triumvirate and staunch supporter of the republican cause during the Civil War; known for his upright, unbending character. After the republican defeat at Pharsalus, the death of Pompey, and the Battle of Thapsus, Cato committed suicide rather than accept pardon from Caesar.

CATULUS: Quintus Lutatius Catulus (149–87 BC), consul in 102, writer and poet, one of the interlocutors in Cicero's dialogue, *De oratore*.

CHARMADAS: Philosopher of the skeptical Academy (ca. 165–after 102 BC); well-known for his oratorical skills and extraordinary memory.

CINNA: Lucius Cornelius Cinna (consul 87–84 BC), ally of Marius and opponent of Sulla during the civil turmoil in Rome during the decade of the 80s BC.

CLARITY: One of the four, traditional "virtues," or qualities of style.

CLODIA: Sister of Publius Clodius Pulcher. According to Cicero, she was the moving force behind the prosecution of Caelius, the young lover who had jilted her. The object of much gossip, she was reputedly free with her favors and even rumored to have had an incestuous relationship with her brother.

CLODIUS: Publius Clodius Pulcher (ca. 92–52 BC), arch-enemy of Cicero. In 62 BC, Clodius was caught, disguised as a woman, at the sacred rites of the Bona

Dea (Good Goddess), at which only women were permitted. In the subsequent trial, Cicero debunked Clodius's alibi; in 58 BC, Clodius instigated Cicero's exile; and in 52, he and Milo and their parties met on the Appian Way and Clodius was killed. Milo was charged and defended by Cicero, who lost the case.

CLOELIUS: Sextus Cloelius, one of Clodius's leading henchmen, responsible for inciting riots and destruction in Rome.

CLUENTIUS: Aulus Cluentius Habitus, defended by Cicero in 66 BC, on a charge of poisoning.

COLLINE: Of or pertaining to the district around the Quirinal Hill. *Collinus* in Latin means "hilly," but when used in reference to Rome, it usually pertains to the Quirinal Hill, one of the seven hills of Rome, and district around it.

COMMONPLACES: Standard arguments about specific issues, or standard argument types, or abstract argument patterns to which the orator can refer and rely upon to build his logical argumentation or appeals to character and emotion.

CONCLUSION: The last of the "parts of a speech," generally devoted to recapitulation and arousal of the audience's emotions.

CONFIRMATIO: See *proof*.

CONSUL: The consuls were Rome's chief magistrates, having both civil and military powers; two were elected annually to hold office for a year.

CORRECTNESS: One of the four traditional "virtues," or qualities of style.

CRASSUS, LUCIUS LICINIUS: The greatest orator of his generation (140–91 BC), one of Cicero's mentors, and the chief interlocutor in his dialogue, *De oratore*.

CRASSUS, MARCUS LICINIUS: One of Rome's richest men (d. 53 BC), consul with Pompey in 70 BC, and a member of the so-called First Triumvirate. He and his army were defeated by the Parthians, and he was murdered by them in 53.

CTESIPHON: Athenian citizen who in 336 BC proposed a crown as a public honor for Demosthenes for his service to the state.

CURIUS: Manius Curius, a party in a famous inheritance case, argued by Lucius Crassus and Quintus Mucius Scaevola Pontifex, involving arguments of the letter versus the spirit of the law.

DEDUCTION: The process of reasoning by which a conclusion follows necessarily from the stated premises; syllogistic reasoning.

DE INVENTIONE (ON INVENTION): Cicero's earliest published work, written when he was still a teenager, on the topic of rhetorical invention; along with the anonymous *Rhetorica ad Herennium*, representative of the sort of handbooks derived from earlier Hellenistic rhetorical theory.

DELIVERY: The fifth of the "activities of the orator," concerning the delivery or presentation of a speech in terms of movements, gestures, facial expression, and voice.

DEMOSTHENES: Most famous of the Greek orators (384–322 BC), whom Cicero considered the finest oratorical model.

DE OFFICIIS (ON MORAL DUTIES): Treatise by Cicero on the subject of moral duties, addressed to his son and written near the end of his life. It has been highly influential on subsequent ages.

DE ORATORE (ON THE IDEAL ORATOR): Cicero's greatest rhetorical treatise, written in three books in 55 BC, and dedicated to his brother Quintus. The treatise is uniquely composed as a dialogue, set in 91 BC, whose chief interlocutors are Crassus and Antonius, endeavoring to describe the ideal orator.

DISPOSITIO: See *arrangement*.

DISTINCTION: One of the four traditional "virtues," or qualities of style, considered the most important; sometimes translated "ornamentation" or "embellishment."

ELOCUTIO: See *style*.

ENNIUS: Famous Roman poet from Rudiae in Calabria (239–169 BC); author of comedies, tragedies, and satire, and of an epic poem, the *Annales*, on the history of Rome up to his time.

ENTHYMEME: A rhetorical syllogism in which either the major or minor premise is implied.

EPICHEIREME: A five-part syllogism in which the major and minor premises are corroborated by further arguments, and then a conclusion is drawn.

EPHORUS: Greek historian from Cyme in Asia Minor (ca. 405–ca. 330 BC) and a pupil of Isocrates.

EQUESTRIAN ORDER: The Roman knights or cavalrymen, the second social class in Rome, consisting of the wealthy who were not senators. Membership required a property qualification of 400,000 sesterces and free birth. By Cicero's time, they did not actually serve as cavalry.

ETHOS: Greek for "character"; along with *logos* and *pathos*, one of the Aristotelian artistic modes of proof, adopted by Cicero in his *De oratore*. Arguments based on the character of the speaker (or his client) and his opponents are used to persuade an audience. The Ciceronian conception of *ethos* is slightly different from Aristotle's.

ETRURIA: A district of northwest Italy.

EXORDIUM: See *prologue*.

FIGURES OF SPEECH AND THOUGHT: Configurations of language that differ from normal and obvious usage; figures of speech usually refer to verbal expression, while figures of thought refer to ideas.

FIMBRIA: Gaius Fimbria, consul in 104 BC, and a powerful orator.

FLAMEN: A priest of one of ancient Rome's deities.

FLAVIUS: Gaius Flavius, presiding judge in the trial of Gnaeus Plancius.

FORMIAE: Town on the west coast of Italy where Cicero was murdered.

FORUM: Public area that was the center of Roman political, ceremonial, legal, and commercial life; site of the Roman Senate house, most criminal and civil trials, public meetings, and many assemblies.

FREGELLANS: Inhabitants of Fragellae, a town allied to Rome, located about 60 miles southeast of the capital. Attempting a revolt in 125 BC, they were destroyed by the Romans.

FUFIUS: Lucius Fufius, prosecutor in the case of Manius Aquillius, who was defended by Antonius in 97 BC.

GRACCHUS: Gaius Sempronius Gracchus, tribune of the people in 123 and 122 BC; talented orator who, like his brother Tiberius, proposed legislation that aimed at relieving the poverty and increasing the power of the people. Despised by the senatorial order, he was murdered during a riot in 121 BC.

GRATTIUS: The prosecutor in the case against Cicero's client, Archias. Nothing further is known about him.

HERACLEA: A city in the south of Italy, located on the river Siris.

HORTENSIUS: Quintus Hortensius Hortalus (114–50 BC); older contemporary of Cicero who held sway in the courts before Cicero's appearance. Defeated by Cicero in the famous case of Verres (70 BC); subsequently, the two orators collaborated on several important cases.

IN CATILINAM: *Against Catiline*, referring to one of the four speeches delivered by Cicero against Catiline and his attempted coup, November–December 63 BC.

INDUCTION: Reasoning from the particular to the general, drawing a conclusion from a particular example and broadening it to include other such cases.

INVENTIO: See *invention*.

INVENTION: The first of the "activities of the orator," involving "discovering" or thinking out the material for a speech.

IPHIGENIA: In mythology, the daughter of Agamemnon and Clytemnestra, sacrificed to secure favorable sailing weather to Troy.

ISOCRATES: Athenian orator, rhetorician, and renowned teacher of rhetoric and oratory, particularly in the areas of style and prose rhythm (436–338 BC).

JUNIUS: Marcus Junius, an advocate who had previously represented Cicero's client, Publius Quinctius; his appointment as legate prevented him from being in court on the day of Cicero's defense speech.

LANUVIUM: A town on the Appian Way, southeast of Rome.

LEPIDUS: Marcus Aemilius Lepidus, consul in 46 and 42 BC; with Antony and Octavian a member of the Second Triumvirate; died in 13 or 12 AD.

LOCI COMMUNES: See *commonplaces*.

LOGOS: Rational argumentation; along with *ethos* and *pathos*, one of the Aristotelian artistic modes of proof, adopted by Cicero in his *De oratore.*

LUCULLUS, LUCIUS LICINIUS: Consul in 74 BC, who waged several successful campaigns against Mithridates, King of Pontus.

LUCULLUS, MARCUS LICINIUS: Brother of Lucius, consul in 73 BC. He was present and testified as a witness on behalf of Archias's enrollment as a citizen at Heraclea.

MANILIAN LAW: The law proposed by the tribune, Gaius Manilius, in 66 BC, granting supreme command to Pompey in the war against Mithridates; the law was supported by Cicero in his speech, *De Lege Manilia.*

MANILIUS: Gaius Manilius, tribune in 66 BC, proposer of a law to grant Pompey supreme command in the war against Mithridates.

MARIUS: Gaius Marius (ca. 157–86 BC); famous general from Cicero's birthplace, Arpinum. Marius reformed the Roman army, was consul seven times, and was involved in a bloody civil war against Sulla in the 80s.

MEMORIA: See *memory*.

MEMORY: The fourth "activity of the orator," consisting of committing a speech to memory.

MENELAUS: In mythology, the king of Sparta, son of Atreus, brother of Agamemnon, and husband of Helen, whom Paris carried off to Troy.

METRODORUS OF SCEPSIS: Rhetorician (ca. 140–71 BC) from Scepsis, in Asia Minor, who was renowned for his prodigious memory.

MILO: Titus Annius Milo, tribune in 57 BC, who worked for Cicero's recall from exile. Charged with Clodius's murder in 52, he was defended by Cicero, but was found guilty and sent into exile.

MITHRIDATES: King of Pontus (Black Sea region), who for decades harassed Roman interests in Asia Minor; finally defeated by Pompey the Great.

NAEVIUS, GNAEUS: Roman poet (fl. ca. 235–205 BC), who wrote comedies, tragedies, and an epic poem on the First Punic War.

NAEVIUS, SEXTUS: Brought suit against Publius Quinctius, whom Cicero defended in 81 BC.

NARRATIO: See *narration*.

NARRATION: The second of the traditional "parts of a speech," the statement of facts (according to the speaker); it should be brief, clear, and persuasive.

NONARTISTIC PROOF: Proof not invented by the speaker's art, for example, written contracts, the testimony of witnesses, and so on.

NORBANUS: Gaius Norbanus, tribune in 103 BC. In 95, he was accused of treason and defended successfully by Marcus Antonius.

ON INVENTION: See *De inventione*.

ON THE IDEAL ORATOR: See *De oratore*.

ON RHETORIC: Treatise by Aristotle, on the art of verbal persuasion.

ORATOR: Rhetorical treatise written by Cicero in the form of a letter (46 BC), directed to Brutus. Cicero maintains that the ideal orator must be a master of the three styles: grand, middle, and plain.

OVATIO: A celebration of a general's exploits, awarded for feats considered worthy, but not meriting a full triumph.

PARTITIO: See *partition*.

PARTITION: A "part of a speech" sometimes included in the standard listing of parts, in which the speaker outlines or lists the points that he intends to cover in his proof.

PATHOS: Greek for "emotion"; along with *logos* and *ethos*, one of the Aristotelian artistic modes of proof, adopted by Cicero in his *De oratore*, by which the speaker, appealing to or stirring the emotions, persuades an audience. The Ciceronian conception of *pathos* is slightly different from that of Aristotle.

PERIODIC STRUCTURE: Sentence structure that is complex and often lengthy, and in which completion of its thought is usually delayed until its end.

PERORATIO: See *conclusion*.

PLANCIUS: Gnaeus Plancius; quaestor in Macedonia in 58 BC, who aided Cicero during his exile. He was later accused of election bribery and successfully defended by Cicero and Hortensius.

PLATO: Athenian philosopher (ca. 429–347 BC), follower of Socrates, founder of the philosophical school known as the Academy, teacher of Aristotle; generally critical of rhetoric.

POLLUX: In mythology, one of the so-called Dioscuri, twin sons of Zeus and Leda; brother of Castor.

POMPEY: Gnaeus Pompeius Magnus (106–48 BC), great general who expelled the pirates from the Mediterranean in 67 BC, and was granted command of Asia Minor in the war against Mithridates in 66; along with Caesar and Crassus, a member of the so-called First Triumvirate. Defeated by Caesar in the Civil War, he was murdered in Egypt in 48 BC.

PRAETOR: In Cicero's time, one of eight Roman magistrates, several of whom presided over a number of the criminal courts. Holding office for a year like other magistrates, the praetor's military and civil powers were second only to those of the consuls.

PRO ARCHIA: Cicero's defense speech on behalf of Archias (see *Archias*), delivered in 62 BC.

PRO CAECINA: Cicero's speech on behalf of Aulus Caecina (see *Caecina*), delivered in 69 BC.

PRO CAELIO: Cicero's defense speech on behalf of Marcus Caelius Rufus (see *Caelius*), delivered in 56 BC.

PRO LEGE MANILIA: Cicero's speech in support of the law proposed by the tribune Manilius, granting Pompey command in the war against Mithridates; also known by the Latin name, *De imperio Cn. Pompei*.

PROLOGUE: First of the traditional "parts of a speech," the introduction, designed to make the audience attentive, receptive, and well-disposed toward the speaker.

PRO MILONE: Cicero's defense speech on behalf of T. Annius Milo (see *Milo*), delivered in 52 BC.

PROOF: One of the traditional "parts of a speech" in which the speaker presents the proof of his case.

PRO PLANCIO: Cicero's defense speech on behalf of Gnaeus Plancius (see *Plancius*), delivered in 54 BC.

PRO QUINCTIO: Cicero's speech on behalf of Publius Quinctius (see *Quinctius*), delivered in 81 BC; his earliest extant speech.

PRO RABIRIO PERDUELLIONIS REO: Cicero's defense speech on behalf of Gaius Rabirius (see *Rabirius*), delivered in 63 BC, his consular year.

PRO ROSCIO AMERINO: Cicero's defense speech on behalf of Roscius of Ameria (see *Roscius of Ameria*), delivered in 80 BC.

PROSE RHYTHM: Metrical rhythm artistically applied to prose by orators. Prose speech was not to be as consistently metrical as poetry, but was expected to have rhythm and cadence, particularly at the end of clauses and sentences.

QUAESTOR: In Cicero's time, one of twenty magistrates, elected annually, who served primarily as financial officers, often attached to senior magistrates.

QUINCTIUS: Publius Quinctius, Cicero's client in a case involving a dispute over property possession.

QUINTILIAN: Marcus Fabius Quintilianus (ca. 35–ca. 95 AD), renowned teacher of rhetoric, author of *Institutio Oratoria (Training of the Orator)*.

RABIRIUS: Gaius Rabirius, Cicero's client in a capital case, actually aimed at assailing the Senate and the powers of the consulship.

REFUTATIO: See *refutation*.

REFUTATION: In rhetorical terms, a subpart of the proof of the speech in which the speaker refutes his opponent's arguments.

RHETORICA AD HERENNIUM (RHETORIC TO HERENNIUS): Anonymous treatise on rhetoric, in four books, addressed to an unknown Gaius Herennius. The manuscript tradition attributes the work wrongly to Cicero, though it is roughly contemporaneous with his *De inventione* and probably shares common sources.

RHODES: The easternmost Greek island in the group known as the Dodecanese, off the southwest coast of Turkey.

ROSCIUS OF AMERIA: Charged with murdering his own father (80 BC), he was defended by Cicero and acquitted.

ROSTRA: The speakers' platform, located in the Roman forum, so-called because it was decorated with the rams of ships (*rostra*) captured in a sea battle in 338 BC.

SCAEVOLA "AUGUR": Quintus Mucius Scaevola the Augur (ca. 168/160–ca. 87 BC), eminent jurist, father-in-law of Crassus the orator, and after Crassus's death, Cicero's chief mentor. He is one of the speakers in Cicero's *De oratore.*

SCAEVOLA "PONTIFEX": Quintus Mucius Scaevola the Pontifex, consul in 95 BC; eminent jurist who spoke opposite Crassus in the famous inheritance case involving Curius, wherein Scaevola upheld the letter versus the spirit of the law.

SENATE: Rome's advisory council composed of ex-magistrates (about 600 in the time of Cicero); its chief purpose was to render advice. Although it technically did not legislate, it was extremely influential in affairs of state.

SIMONIDES OF CEOS: Greek lyric poet from the island of Ceos (557–468 BC) who was believed to have invented the art of memory.

SOCRATES: Famous Athenian philosopher and public figure (469–399 BC); Plato and Xenophon number among his followers.

STATEMENT OF FACTS: See *narration*.

STATUS: One of four "stances of argument" chosen to address the matter under judgment in a judicial case. Classifying the stance of argument is one of the chief elements of "invention," the first activity of the orator.

STYLE: One of the standard "activities of the orator," consisting of putting the material of a speech into words.

SULLA: Lucius Cornelius Sulla "Felix" (138–78 BC), powerful general and leading aristocrat, rival of Marius during the tumultuous decade of the 80s; victor in the bloody civil war in 82, relying on confiscation and proscription to restore order. Subsequently as dictator, he enacted many laws, increasing the power of the Senate and reforming and reorganizing the courts and judicial procedure. After completion of his reforms, he retired to private life in 79, and died shortly thereafter.

SULPICIUS: Publius Sulpicius Rufus (124–88 BC), tribune of the people in 88 BC; one of the interlocutors in Cicero's dialogue, *De oratore.*

SYLLOGISM: A form of deductive reasoning consisting of a major premise, a minor premise, and a conclusion.

THEOPHRASTUS: Greek philosopher (ca. 371–286 BC), pupil of Aristotle, and author of many scientific, philosophical, and rhetorical works.

GLOSSARY

THEOPOMPUS: Greek historian from the island of Chios (378–ca. 320 BC), student of Isocrates, and author of many historical works.

TOPICS: See *commonplaces*.

TRIBUNE (OF THE PEOPLE): Roman magistrate charged with the protection of the people; in Cicero's time, ten tribunes were elected annually to hold office for one year. Tribunes could veto acts of magistrates, laws, resolutions of the Senate, and elections, and could summon meetings and propose laws.

TUSCULUM: Town situated in the mountains southeast of Rome, about 10 miles from the city; the location of Cicero's favorite country estate.

ULYSSES: Latin name for Odysseus, in mythology, son of Laertes, king of Ithaca, hero of the Trojan War, subject of Homer's *Odyssey*.

WAR WITH THE ALLIES: Also known as the "Social" or "Marsic War," waged between Rome and her Italian allies from 91–87 BC; resulted in the granting of citizenship to the Italian allies south of the Po River.

XENOPHON: Athenian general and writer (ca. 430–after 355 BC), follower of Socrates, author of, among other works, the *Anabasis*, *Hellenica*, and *Memorabilia*.

FURTHER READING

Primary Sources

All of Cicero's rhetorical works (including the anonymous *Rhetorica ad Herennium*) and speeches are available in English translation from the Loeb Classical Library (Cambridge, MA: Harvard University Press/London: William Heinemann).

The most up-to-date translation (including notes, glossary, and appendices) of Cicero's *De oratore* is James M. May and Jakob Wisse, *Cicero: On the Ideal Orator* (New York: Oxford University Press, 2001).

Other collections of selected translated speeches:

Berry, D. H. *Defence Speeches.* Oxford: Oxford University Press, 2000.

Grant, Michael. *Cicero: Murder Trials.* New York: Penguin, 1975.

———. *Cicero: Selected Political Speeches.* New York: Penguin, 1969.

Kaster, Robert A. *Cicero: Speech on Behalf of Publius Sestius.* Oxford: Oxford University Press, 2006.

Shackleton Bailey, D. R. *Cicero: Back from Exile: Six Speeches upon His Return.* Chicago: American Philological Association, 1991.

———. *Cicero's Philippics.* Chapel Hill: University of North Carolina Press, 1986.

Secondary Sources

Included here is a selection of scholarly works on ancient rhetoric and oratory in general, and Cicero and Ciceronian rhetoric and oratory in particular.

Connolly, Joy. *The State of Speech: Rhetoric and Political Thought at Rome.* Princeton, NJ: Princeton University Press, 2007.

Craig, Christopher P. *Form as Argument in Cicero's Speeches: A Study of Dilemma.* Atlanta: Scholars Press, 1993.

Dominik, William, and Hall, Jon, eds. *A Companion to Roman Rhetoric.* Oxford: Blackwell, 2007.

Dugan, John. *Making a New Man: Ciceronian Self-Fashioning in the Rhetorical Works.* Oxford: Oxford University Press, 2005.

Fantham, Elaine. *The Roman World of Cicero's* De oratore. New York: Oxford University Press, 2004.

Hall, Jon. *Cicero's Use of Judicial Theater.* Ann Arbor: University of Michigan Press, 2014.

FURTHER READING

Kennedy, George A. *The Art of Rhetoric in the Roman World, 300 BC–AD 300*. Princeton, NJ: Princeton University Press, 1972

———. *A New History of Classical Rhetoric.* Princeton, NJ: Princeton University Press, 1994.

May, James M. *Trials of Character: The Eloquence of Ciceronian Ethos.* Chapel Hill and London: University of North Carolina Press, 1988.

May, James M., ed. *Brill's Companion to Cicero: Rhetoric and Oratory.* Leiden: E. J. Brill, 2002.

McKendrick, Paul. *The Speeches of Cicero.* London: Duckworth, 1995.

Mitchell, T. N. *Cicero: The Ascending Years*. New Haven, CT: Yale University Press, 1979.

———. *Cicero: The Senior Statesman.* New Haven, CT: Yale University Press, 1991.

Powell, Jonathan, and Paterson, Jeremy, eds. *Cicero the Advocate.* Oxford: Oxford University Press, 2004.

Rawson, Elizabeth. *Cicero: A Portrait.* London: Allen Lane, 1975.

Shackleton Bailey, D. R. *Cicero.* London: Duckworth, 1971.

Steel, C.E.W. *Cambridge Companion to Cicero.* Cambridge: Cambridge University Press, 2013.

———. *Cicero, Rhetoric, and Empire.* Oxford: Oxford University Press, 2001.

———. *Roman Oratory.* Cambridge: Cambridge University Press, 2006.

245

Vasaly, Ann. *Representations: Images of the World in Ciceronian Oratory.* Berkeley: University of California Press, 1993.

Wisse, Jakob. *Ethos and Pathos from Aristotle to Cicero.* Amsterdam: Hakkert, 1989.

TEXT CREDITS

The Origins of Eloquent and Persuasive Speech

Nature, Art, Practice

De inventione 1.2–3 (reprinted by permission of the publishers and the Trustees of the Loeb Classical Library from *Cicero: Volume II*, Loeb Classical Library Volume 386, trans. H. M. Hubbell, Cambridge, MA: Harvard University Press, 1976, pp. 4, 6, 8. Loeb Classical Library ® is a registered trademark of the President and Fellows of Harvard College); *De oratore* 1.30–34 (by permission of Bibliotheca Scriptorum Graecorum et Romanorum Teubneriana: from *M. Tulli Ciceronis: De oratore*, ed. Kazimierz F. Kumaniecki, Leipzig: B. G. Teubner Verlagsgesellschaft (De Gruyter), 1969, pp. 12–14, as adapted by J. M. May and J. Wisse, *Cicero: On the Ideal Orator*, Oxford and New York:

Oxford University Press, 2001); *De oratore* 2.232 (by permission of Bibliotheca Scriptorum Graecorum et Romanorum Teubneriana: from *M. Tulli Ciceronis: De oratore*, ed. Kazimierz F. Kumaniecki, Leipzig: B. G. Teubner Verlagsgesellschaft (De Gruyter), 1969, pp. 202–3, as adapted by J. M. May and J. Wisse, *Cicero: On the Ideal Orator*, Oxford and New York: Oxford University Press, 2001).

Rhetoric and Truth

De inventione 1.1 (reprinted by permission of the publishers and the Trustees of the Loeb Classical Library from *Cicero: Volume II*, Loeb Classical Library Volume 386, trans. H. M. Hubbell, Cambridge, MA: Harvard University Press, 1976, pp. 2, 4. Loeb Classical Library ® is a registered trademark of the President and Fellows of Harvard College); *De officiis* 2.51 (by permission of Oxford University Press, www.oup.com: from *M. Tulli Ciceronis De officiis*, ed. M. Winterbottom, Oxford: Oxford University Press, 1994, pp. 90–91).

The Parts of Rhetoric, or Activities of the Orator

Invention: Identifying and Classifying the Question at Issue According to the Stance of Argument, and Discovering the Sources of Proof

Status *(Stances of Argument)*

De inventione 1.10 (reprinted by permission of the publishers and the Trustees of the Loeb Classical Library from *Cicero: Volume II*, Loeb Classical Library Volume 386, trans. H. M. Hubbell, Cambridge, MA: Harvard University Press, 1976, pp. 20, 22. Loeb Classical Library ® is a registered trademark of the President and Fellows of Harvard College).

The Sources of Proof

De oratore 2.114–17 (by permission of Bibliotheca Scriptorum Graecorum et Romanorum Teubneriana: from *M. Tulli Ciceronis: De oratore*, ed. Kazimierz F. Kumaniecki, Leipzig: B. G. Teubner Verlagsgesellschaft (De Gruyter), 1969, pp. 150–51, as adapted by J. M. May and J. Wisse, *Cicero: On the Ideal Orator*, Oxford and New

York: Oxford University Press, 2001); *De oratore* 2.145–47 (by permission of Bibliotheca Scriptorum Graecorum et Romanorum Teubneriana: from *M. Tulli Ciceronis: De oratore*, ed. Kazimierz F. Kumaniecki, Leipzig: B. G. Teubner Verlagsgesellschaft (De Gruyter), 1969, pp. 163–64, as adapted by J. M. May and J. Wisse, *Cicero: On the Ideal Orator*, Oxford and New York: Oxford University Press, 2001).

LOGOS (RATIONAL ARGUMENTATION)

De inventione 1.51–52 (reprinted by permission of the publishers and the Trustees of the Loeb Classical Library from *Cicero: Volume II*, Loeb Classical Library Volume 386, trans. H. M. Hubbell, Cambridge, MA: Harvard University Press, 1976, pp. 92, 94. Loeb Classical Library ® is a registered trademark of the President and Fellows of Harvard College); *De inventione* 1.58–59 (reprinted by permission of the publishers and the Trustees of the Loeb Classical Library from *Cicero: Volume II*, Loeb Classical Library Volume 386, trans. H. M. Hubbell, Cambridge, MA: Harvard University Press, 1976, pp. 100, 102. Loeb Classical Library ® is a registered trademark of the President and Fellows of Harvard College).

ETHOS (ARGUMENT BASED ON CHARACTER)

De oratore 2.182–84 (by permission of Bibliotheca Scriptorum Graecorum et Romanorum Teubneriana: from *M. Tulli Ciceronis: De oratore*, ed. Kazimierz F. Kumaniecki, Leipzig: B. G. Teubner Verlagsgesellschaft (De Gruyter), 1969, pp. 177–79, as adapted by J. M. May and J. Wisse, *Cicero: On the Ideal Orator*, Oxford and New York: Oxford University Press, 2001); *Pro Roscio Amerino* 75 (by permission of Oxford University Press, www.oup.com: from *M. Tulli Ciceronis Orationes: Pro Sex. Roscio, De Imperio Cn. Pompei, Pro Cluentio, In Catilinam, Pro Murena, Pro Caelio*, ed. A. C. Clark, Oxford: Oxford University Press, 1970, one page of text not numbered); *In Catilinam* 2.22–25 (by permission of Oxford University Press, www.oup.com: from *M. Tulli Ciceronis Orationes: Pro Sex. Roscio, De Imperio Cn. Pompei, Pro Cluentio, In Catilinam, Pro Murena, Pro Caelio*, ed. A. C. Clark, Oxford: Oxford University Press, 1970, three pages of text not numbered).

PATHOS (ARGUMENT BASED ON EMOTIONAL APPEAL)

De oratore 2.185–87 (by permission of Bibliotheca Scriptorum Graecorum et Romanorum

Teubneriana: from *M. Tulli Ciceronis: De oratore*, ed. Kazimierz F. Kumaniecki, Leipzig: B. G. Teubner Verlagsgesellschaft (De Gruyter), 1969, pp. 179–80, as adapted by J. M. May and J. Wisse, *Cicero: On the Ideal Orator*, Oxford and New York: Oxford University Press, 2001); *De oratore* 2.194–96 (by permission of Bibliotheca Scriptorum Graecorum et Romanorum Teubneriana: from *M. Tulli Ciceronis: De oratore*, ed. Kazimierz F. Kumaniecki, Leipzig: B. G. Teubner Verlagsgesellschaft (De Gruyter), 1969, pp. 184–85, as adapted by J. M. May and J. Wisse, *Cicero: On the Ideal Orator*, Oxford and New York: Oxford University Press, 2001); *Pro Plancio* 101–4 (by permission of Oxford University Press, www.oup.com: from *M. Tulli Ciceronis Orationes: Pro Tullio, Pro Fonteio, Pro Sulla, Pro Archia, Pro Plancio, Pro Scauro*, ed. A. C. Clark, Oxford: Oxford University Press, 1968, two pages of text not numbered).

Arrangement

De oratore 2.307–12 (by permission of Bibliotheca Scriptorum Graecorum et Romanorum Teubneriana: from *M. Tulli Ciceronis: De oratore*, ed. Kazimierz F. Kumaniecki, Leipzig: B. G. Teubner Verlagsgesellschaft (De Gruyter), 1969, pp. 235–37, as adapted by J. M. May and J. Wisse, *Cicero: On the Ideal Orator*, Oxford and New York: Oxford University Press, 2001).

Introduction or Prologue (*Latin* Exordium)

Pro P. Quinctio 1–8, 10 (by permission of Oxford University Press, www.oup.com: from *M. Tulli Ciceronis Orationes: Pro P. Quinctio, Pro Q. Roscio Comoedo, Pro A. Caecina, De Lege Agraria, Contra Rullum, Pro C. Rabirio Perduellionis Reo, Pro L. Flacco, In L. Pisonem, Pro C. Rabirio Postumo*, ed. A. C. Clark, Oxford: Oxford University Press, 1966, four pages of text not numbered).

Narration or Statement of Facts (*Latin* Narratio)

Pro Milone 23–29 (by permission of Oxford University Press, www.oup.com: from *M. Tulli Ciceronis Orationes: Pro Milone, Pro Marcello, Pro Ligario, Pro Rege Deiotaro, Philippicae I–XIV*, ed. A. C. Clark, Oxford: Oxford University Press, 1970, three pages of text not numbered).

Confirmation or Proof
(*Latin* Confirmatio)

De Inventione 1.34, 37, 44, 46 (reprinted by permission of the publishers and the Trustees of the Loeb Classical Library from *Cicero: Volume II*, Loeb Classical Library Volume 386, trans. H. M. Hubbell, Cambridge, MA: Harvard University Press, 1976, pp. 68, 74, 82, 84, 86. Loeb Classical Library ® is a registered trademark of the President and Fellows of Harvard College); *Pro Milone* 52–55 (by permission of Oxford University Press, www.oup.com: from *M. Tulli Ciceronis Orationes: Pro Milone, Pro Marcello, Pro Ligario, Pro Rege Deiotaro, Philippicae I–XIV*, ed. A. C. Clark, Oxford: Oxford University Press, 1970, three pages of text not numbered).

Refutation (*Latin* Refutatio)

De oratore 2.331 (by permission of Bibliotheca Scriptorum Graecorum et Romanorum Teubneriana: from *M. Tulli Ciceronis: De oratore*, ed. Kazimierz F. Kumaniecki, Leipzig: B. G. Teubner Verlagsgesellschaft (De Gruyter), 1969, pp. 245–46, as adapted by J. M. May and J. Wisse,

Cicero: On the Ideal Orator, Oxford and New York: Oxford University Press, 2001); *De inventione* 1.79 (reprinted by permission of the publishers and the Trustees of the Loeb Classical Library from *Cicero: Volume II*, Loeb Classical Library Volume 386, trans. H. M. Hubbell, Cambridge, MA: Harvard University Press, 1976, p. 124. Loeb Classical Library ® is a registered trademark of the President and Fellows of Harvard College); *Pro Archia* 8–11 (by permission of Oxford University Press, www.oup.com: from *M. Tulli Ciceronis Orationes: Pro Tullio, Pro Fonteio, Pro Sulla, Pro Archia, Pro Plancio, Pro Scauro*, ed. A. C. Clark, Oxford: Oxford University Press, 1968, three pages of text not numbered).

Conclusion or Epilogue
(*Latin* Conclusio *or* Peroratio)

Pro Caelio 70, 77–80 (by permission of Oxford University Press, www.oup.com: from *M. Tulli Ciceronis Orationes: Pro Sex. Roscio, De Imperio Cn. Pompei, Pro Cluentio, In Catilinam, Pro Murena, Pro Caelio*, ed. A. C. Clark, Oxford: Oxford University Press, 1970, five pages of text not numbered).

Style

De oratore 3.19, 22–24 (by permission of Bibliotheca Scriptorum Graecorum et Romanorum Teubneriana: from *M. Tulli Ciceronis: De oratore*, ed. Kazimierz F. Kumaniecki, Leipzig: B. G. Teubner Verlagsgesellschaft (De Gruyter), 1969, pp. 270–72, as adapted by J. M. May and J. Wisse, *Cicero: On the Ideal Orator*, Oxford and New York: Oxford University Press, 2001); *De oratore* 3.34–36 (by permission of Bibliotheca Scriptorum Graecorum et Romanorum Teubneriana: from *M. Tulli Ciceronis: De oratore*, ed. Kazimierz F. Kumaniecki, Leipzig: B. G. Teubner Verlagsgesellschaft (De Gruyter), 1969, pp. 275–76, as adapted by J. M. May and J. Wisse, *Cicero: On the Ideal Orator*, Oxford and New York: Oxford University Press, 2001).

Virtues of Style

CORRECTNESS AND CLARITY

De oratore 3.37–41, 48–49 (by permission of Bibliotheca Scriptorum Graecorum et Romanorum Teubneriana: from *M. Tulli Ciceronis: De oratore*, ed. Kazimierz F. Kumaniecki, Leipzig: B. G. Teubner Verlagsgesellschaft (De Gruyter),

1969, pp. 277–78, 280, as adapted by J. M. May and J. Wisse, *Cicero: On the Ideal Orator*, Oxford and New York: Oxford University Press, 2001).

DISTINCTION (ORNAMENTATION)

De oratore 3.96–101 (by permission of Bibliotheca Scriptorum Graecorum et Romanorum Teubneriana: from *M. Tulli Ciceronis: De oratore*, ed. Kazimierz F. Kumaniecki, Leipzig: B. G. Teubner Verlagsgesellschaft (De Gruyter), 1969, pp. 298–300, as adapted by J. M. May and J. Wisse, *Cicero: On the Ideal Orator*, Oxford and New York: Oxford University Press, 2001).

APPROPRIATENESS

De oratore 3.210–12 (by permission of Bibliotheca Scriptorum Graecorum et Romanorum Teubneriana: from *M. Tulli Ciceronis: De oratore*, ed. Kazimierz F. Kumaniecki, Leipzig: B. G. Teubner Verlagsgesellschaft (De Gruyter), 1969, pp. 351–52, as adapted by J. M. May and J. Wisse, *Cicero: On the Ideal Orator*, Oxford and New York: Oxford University Press, 2001); *Orator* 70–74 (by permission of Oxford University Press, www.oup.com: from *M. Tulli Ciceronis Rhetorica, Volume II: Brutus, Orator, De Optimo*

Perduellionis Reo, Pro L. Flacco, In L. Pisonem, Pro C. Rabirio Postumo, ed. A. C. Clark, Oxford: Oxford University Press, 1966, three pages of text not numbered).

Memory

De oratore 2.351–360 (by permission of Bibliotheca Scriptorum Graecorum et Romanorum Teubneriana: from *M. Tulli Ciceronis: De oratore*, ed. Kazimierz F. Kumaniecki, Leipzig: B. G. Teubner Verlagsgesellschaft (De Gruyter), 1969, pp. 253–57, as adapted by J. M. May and J. Wisse, *Cicero: On the Ideal Orator*, Oxford and New York: Oxford University Press, 2001).

Delivery

Brutus 142 (by permission of Oxford University Press, www.oup.com: from *M. Tulli Ciceronis Rhetorica, Volume II: Brutus, Orator, De Optimo Genere Oratorum, Partitiones Oratoriae, Topica*, ed. A. S. Wilkins, Oxford: Oxford University Press, 1970, two pages of text not numbered); *De oratore* 3.213–27 (by permission of Bibliotheca Scriptorum Graecorum et Romanorum Teubneriana: from *M. Tulli Ciceronis: De oratore*, ed. Kazimierz F. Kumaniecki, Leipzig: B. G. Teubner Verlagsgesellschaft (De Gruyter), 1969, pp. 352–61, as adapted by J. M. May and J. Wisse, *Cicero: On the Ideal Orator*, Oxford and New York, Oxford University Press, 2001).

THE VALUE OF IMITATING GOOD MODELS OF SPEAKING

De oratore 2.88–92, 96 (by permission of Bibliotheca Scriptorum Graecorum et Romanorum Teubneriana: from *M. Tulli Ciceronis: De oratore*, ed. Kazimierz F. Kumaniecki, Leipzig: B. G. Teubner Verlagsgesellschaft (De Gruyter), 1969, pp. 139–41, 143, as adapted by J. M. May and J. Wisse, *Cicero: On the Ideal Orator*, Oxford and New York: Oxford University Press, 2001).

THE VALUE OF WRITING TO PREPARE FOR EFFECTIVE SPEAKING

De oratore 1.149–55 (by permission of Bibliotheca Scriptorum Graecorum et Romanorum Teubneriana: from *M. Tulli Ciceronis: De oratore*, ed. Kazimierz F. Kumaniecki, Leipzig: B. G. Teubner Verlagsgesellschaft (De Gruyter), 1969, pp. 56–58, as adapted by J. M. May and

J. Wisse, *Cicero: On the Ideal Orator*, Oxford and New York: Oxford University Press, 2001).

THE REQUIREMENTS AND EDUCATION OF THE IDEAL SPEAKER

De oratore 1.6–20 (by permission of Bibliotheca Scriptorum Graecorum et Romanorum Teubneriana: from *M. Tulli Ciceronis: De oratore*, ed. Kazimierz F. Kumaniecki, Leipzig: B. G. Teubner Verlagsgesellschaft (De Gruyter), 1969, pp. 3–9, as adapted by J. M. May and J. Wisse, *Cicero: On the Ideal Orator*, Oxford and New York: Oxford University Press, 2001).

The following passages are excerpted from *Cicero: On the Ideal Orator*, translated, with introduction, notes, appendixes, glossary, and indexes, by James M. May and Jakob Wisse (New York and Oxford, 2001); they are reproduced here by permission of Oxford University Press, USA © Oxford University Press:

1.6–20 (pp. 58–62); 1.30–34 (pp. 64–65); 1.149–55 (pp. 91–92); 2.88–96 (pp. 146–48); 2.114–17 (pp. 153–54); 2.145–47 (p. 161); 2.182–84 (pp. 171–72);

2.185–87 (p. 172); 2.194–96 (pp. 174–75); 2.232 (p. 185); 2.307–12 (pp. 208–9); 2.331 (p. 214); 2.351–60 (pp. 219–21); 3.19, 22–24 (pp. 230–31); 3.34–36 (p. 234); 3.37–41, 48–49 (pp. 235, 237); 3.96–101 (pp. 253–54); 3.210–12 (p. 290); 3.213–27 (pp. 290–96).